T0381442

THE ULTIMATE TEACHER

DISCOVERING THE LESSONS OF LIFE AND LOVE
THROUGH A JOURNEY OF RESILIENCE

BLANCA MARTINI

BALBOA.PRESS
A DIVISION OF HAY HOUSE

Balboa Press books may be ordered through booksellers or by contacting:

Balboa Press
A Division of Hay House
1663 Liberty Drive
Bloomington, IN 47403
www.balboapress.com
844-682-1282

Because of the dynamic nature of the Internet, any web addresses or links contained in this book may have changed since publication and may no longer be valid. The views expressed in this work are solely those of the author and do not necessarily reflect the views of the publisher, and the publisher hereby disclaims any responsibility for them.

The author of this book does not dispense medical advice or prescribe the use of any technique as a form of treatment for physical, emotional, or medical problems without the advice of a physician, either directly or indirectly. The intent of the author is only to offer information of a general nature to help you in your quest for emotional and spiritual well-being. In the event you use any of the information in this book for yourself, which is your constitutional right, the author and the publisher assume no responsibility for your actions.

Any people depicted in stock imagery provided by Getty Images are models, and such images are being used for illustrative purposes only. Certain stock imagery © Getty Images.

Print information available on the last page.

ISBN: 979-8-7652-5909-2 (sc)
ISBN: 979-8-7652-5908-5 (e)

Balboa Press rev. date: 01/09/2025

Preface

The journey of writing this book began many years ago. Writing has always been a passion of mine, and countless people encouraged me to put pen to paper, insisting that my collection of interesting and entertaining stories deserved to be shared in a book.

Yet, despite all the enthusiasm, the book never materialized. There was always a reason to delay—whether it was the belief that I needed more creative writing classes or, even after taking those classes, the lingering doubt that my work was good enough to publish. I constantly compare my writing to the authors I admired, and in doing so, I convinced myself that my voice wasn't worthy. As I've since learned, comparison is the death of creativity.

Then everything changed when a life-threatening event shook me to my core. The prospect of never finishing this book became a very real possibility, and with that, the urgency to bring it to completion hit me hard. Suddenly, I realized I had something more meaningful to share—a message deeper than mere anecdotes. And for the first time, I had the time. Retirement, along with the isolation forced by a weakened immune system, provided me with the tools I had long lacked: time, discipline, dedication, and most importantly, intention.

What once felt trivial, or even arrogant to consider publishing, now felt purposeful. This memoir wasn't just a collection of stories—it had meaning, and perhaps even an audience.

I dedicate this work to my children, who have always been the guiding light of my life. My hope is that this memoir not only reminds you of where and whom you come from but also helps shed light on the whys, whats, and how's of the journey that shaped our lives.

With love and gratitude.

PART 1

CHAPTER 1

"Crisis creates the tension needed to liberate
life into a higher way of being."

- William Meader, Supernal Light

On February 3, 2021, I received the diagnosis that would change everything: Acute Myeloblastic Leukemia, or AML, more specifically AML M5. This news followed a bone marrow extraction test on January 27, 2021, though the symptoms had started months earlier, in October 2020. At first, I dismissed the signs as post-move fatigue, but they quickly became too alarming to ignore. I was experiencing intense night sweats— worse than anything I had gone through during menopause— along with joint pain and swelling. Most disturbingly, I noticed a strange discoloration of the veins in my ankles. It happened on the very day I moved into my apartment in Guatemala City, and from that moment, I knew something serious was happening inside me.

AML is a form of cancer that attacks the blood and bone marrow, affecting red blood cells, white blood cells, and platelets. It primarily impacts adults, and the likelihood of developing it increases with age. The term "acute" refers to the disease's rapid progression. AML can cause a drastic decline in health over a short period, and mine had already begun.

Upon hearing the diagnosis, my immediate reaction wasn't fear or anger but acceptance. This wasn't resignation or defeat—acceptance felt like the only place where real change could begin. I had learned over time, particularly through the teachings of Eckhart Tolle, that what we resist persists. His words echoed in my mind, reminding me that resistance only breeds suffering. Instead of asking, "Why me?" my thoughts went to the Serenity Prayer: "God, grant me the serenity to accept the things I cannot change, the courage to change the things I can, and the wisdom to know the difference."

In that moment, a deep sense of understanding washed over me. I realized that this diagnosis had arrived not as a curse but as a Great Teacher—the Ultimate Teacher. The question that arose wasn't "How do I get through this?" but rather, "What am I to learn from this?"

As Michael Meade, host of the *Living Myth* podcast, says, "An illness stops us in our course, and then can be a wake-up call, if we allow the body to teach us what's going on." I knew this was my wake-up call, an opportunity to listen to what my body, and perhaps LIFE itself, was trying to tell me.

Acceptance, I understood, is not about giving up. It's about releasing resistance—letting go of the judgments, fears, and criticisms that only serve to lock us in anxiety, despair, and denial. I had spent far too much time in that cycle, and I was ready to break free. Acceptance, as I saw it, was a sword that cut through all of that mental clutter. It allowed me to relax, see things clearly, and respond with grace instead of panic.

This idea of acceptance as a path to peace is also explored in *The Book of Joy,* where the Dalai Lama speaks about the eight pillars of joy—four qualities of the mind and four of the heart. The four pillars of the mind are perspective, humility, humor, and acceptance. The four pillars of the heart are forgiveness, gratitude, compassion, and generosity. I found solace in the idea that acceptance is not just the final pillar of the mind but also a gateway to the heart's journey, starting with forgiveness.

And forgiveness was precisely what I needed—both for others and for myself. The diagnosis forced me to confront years of unspoken resentments and unhealed wounds. I had to forgive those who had wronged me, but even more crucially, I had to forgive myself for all the ways I had held myself back. This illness, terrifying as it was, had given me the gift of clarity. It showed me that forgiveness and healing are not only possible but necessary if I was to emerge from this with a deeper sense of self and purpose.

This was the lesson my Ultimate Teacher was imparting: that life, even in its harshest moments, is still full of opportunities for growth, healing, and transformation. Acceptance wasn't just a passive surrender—it was an active choice, a way of reclaiming my life from fear and moving forward with a heart full of compassion, for others and for myself.

When my adult children, all now leading their own busy lives, heard of my definitive diagnosis, they immediately gathered for a Zoom meeting. Ever since the onset of the COVID-19 pandemic, Zoom had become our virtual living room, the space where we conducted all our social interactions. In fact, I had just celebrated Christmas with them via Zoom, as they were all residing in different parts of the United States. It's in moments like these that technology proves to be invaluable. Naturally, they were all deeply worried, and each of them reacted in their own distinct way.

My oldest son, Canche, the bedrock of my existence, was facing his own set of challenges. He and his long-term life partner, Ricky, were in the midst of a difficult decision— whether to purchase their first home. They had done all the necessary preparations, filled out the paperwork, and secured a loan for a mortgage. But the stress of the situation was compounded by the fact that they were considering moving to

San Antonio, Texas, where his partner was from, rather than staying in Chicago, where they had built their life together for the past 18 years. The prospect of relocating out of state and taking on the responsibility of homeownership weighed heavily on him.

My daughter, Myriam, who lives in South Bend, Indiana, responded in a way that completely took me by surprise. Though she isn't religious—she actually cringes at the very mention of the word "God," a word that holds such heavy, complex connotations for so many—she went to the Grotto at Notre Dame to light a candle for me. The weight of that gesture, especially given her feelings toward the idea of "God," moved me deeply. It was a powerful sign of how much she cared, transcending her discomfort with religion. I was touched beyond words. She even began immediately making arrangements to renew her passport so she could come to my aid.

At the same time, my youngest son, Danny, had returned to his childhood home, living with his father as he tried to regain his footing and find a sense of stability in his own life. Life had dealt him his own set of challenges, and he was navigating the often painful process of rebuilding. It was clear that he was struggling, unable to fully extend himself to anyone else while facing his own inner battles. But despite his own burdens, he still found a way to be with me during the remainder of my chemotherapy treatment. His presence was a quiet testament to his love and his desire to support me in the best way he could. I understood that sometimes, simply being there—even when life feels overwhelming—is an act of love in itself. We both were dealing with different storms, but in those moments, we weathered them together, each of us giving what we could, when we could.

Each of my children was grappling with the news in their

own way, but we were all united by a shared sense of worry and fear…and also HOPE.

In the end, my two eldest children made the decision to fly to Guatemala to be by my side during my first hospitalization and round of chemotherapy. They handled all the necessary arrangements and arrived just a few days before I was admitted to Hospital Centro Médico—the very same hospital where I had given birth to all three of them, and where my father had once played a pivotal role as a key member of the medical community. Because of my family's long-standing ties to the hospital, and with my brother also being a physician, not a single doctor charged me for their care. I was only responsible for the hospital and medication fees, which were already significant on their own.

Once again, Canche, along with Ricky—who has truly become like another son to me—stepped up and shouldered the financial burden. Their generosity and unwavering support overwhelmed me. Words will never be enough to express the depth of my gratitude. In the midst of such a challenging time, I was surrounded by blessings—an incredible gift of care, love, and financial assistance that I will forever be thankful for.

None of us knew what to expect. We were all shaken, terrified of the unknown. Chemotherapy is a notoriously unpredictable and aggressive treatment, designed to kill—its very nature brutal. No one, not even the doctors, could say with certainty how my body would respond. Despite all the studies, the charts, the percentages, and averages, the outcome was still unclear. Because in the end, we are not just statistics or numbers on a page. We are individual human beings, each with a unique composition. And in that uncertainty, we found ourselves bracing for whatever might come, hopeful yet deeply aware of the fragility of life.

The treatment I underwent was nothing short of aggressive and unrelenting. It felt like my body was being thrust into a whirlwind of medical interventions, each more intense than the last. Over the course of that first treatment, I endured three bone marrow biopsies and four separate hospitalizations. The chemotherapy was relentless—administered intravenously, 24/7, in a cocktail designed to eradicate the cancer at any cost. This included two rounds of "induction" chemotherapy, two "consolidation" phases, and an outpatient intravenous "maintenance" cycle. Following this, I endured four months of oral chemotherapy with Purinethol and Methotrexate, in a grueling cycle of 21 days on, followed by a mere 7 days off. On top of all that, I had to undergo several rounds of Filgrastim injections, which were administered subcutaneously around my belly button, along with four blood transfusions during my second induction and consolidation phase in the hospital.

Medically, the chemotherapy protocol I was placed on was referred to as a "7 + 3 schematic," a regimen based on two powerful drugs: Doxorubicin and Cytosar. The logic behind this treatment is that Cytarabine (Cytosar) is administered intravenously for 7 days straight, while Doxorubicin is introduced for 3 days of short infusions during both the induction and consolidation phases. It's a formulaic yet brutal combination, aimed at eradicating the cancer cells.

Yet, for all its scientific precision, the side effects were devastating. I was warned that these drugs would lower my white blood cell count, leaving me vulnerable to infections— an especially terrifying prospect during the peak of the COVID-19 pandemic. The painful mouth sores that followed made it difficult to eat or speak, while constant nausea was only barely controlled by anti-sickness medication. Fatigue settled in like an unwelcome guest, lingering long after each round of chemotherapy had ended. Joint pain, ironically, was both a symptom of the disease and a side effect of the treatment—a cruel twist of fate that made daily life even harder to bear.

One of the most toxic effects of Cytarabine is its impact

on bone marrow, suppressing its function and leading to leukopenia, thrombocytopenia, and anemia. Leukopenia, a condition where the body doesn't produce enough disease-fighting white blood cells, left me constantly exposed to the risk of infection. White blood cells are produced in the bone marrow, which is why I was given Filgrastim injections to help stimulate my body's production of new cells. Filgrastim is a synthetic version of a naturally occurring substance in the body called a colony-stimulating factor, which is designed to help the bone marrow recover by producing new white blood cells.

It felt paradoxical to me that the very treatment meant to save my life was also attacking the core of my body's ability to protect itself. It seemed almost nonsensical—the chemotherapy weakened my immune system and suppressed my bone marrow, while I was simultaneously being injected with drugs to counteract those very effects. But, like a faithful patient who trusted the wisdom of Western medicine, I didn't question the process. After all, this was the path I had chosen, the one I had been raised to believe in. And so, I submitted myself fully to the regimen, following each step with the hope that somehow, despite the hardship, it would lead to my recovery.

Through it all, I clung to the belief that enduring this grueling process was my best chance at survival. Even as my body weakened, and as each new side effect piled onto the next, I kept my focus on the long-term goal: getting back to wholeness. There was no room for doubt; I simply had to trust that every needle, every round of chemo, and every transfusion was working in concert to give me a future.

After the first induction—a grueling eight days of continuous chemotherapy and hospitalization—I was finally allowed to return home. While the hospital had been the epicenter of my treatment, it quickly became apparent that being in the sterile, impersonal environment of the hospital posed far more risks than the comfort of my own apartment.

There, under the loving watch of my children, I was able to weather the storm of side effects with much more grace and resilience than I ever could have within the hospital walls.

When the first waves of discomfort from the chemo began to settle in, I found solace in being surrounded by my children's care. They were vigilant, ensuring I was as comfortable as possible during each painful moment. Every ache, every wave of nausea, every discomfort that chemotherapy hurled at me was met with their loving support. It helped me to endure it all with a sense of dignity, despite the immense physical and emotional toll.

Then came the moment I dreaded—the loss of my hair. It was as if losing my hair symbolized the most visible mark of my struggle. I knew it was inevitable, but nothing could have prepared me for the reality. As I stood in the shower, feeling the weight of my hair falling in clumps down my back, clogging the drain, I let out a cry that was raw and primal. The grief I felt at that moment was unexpected, but deeply real.

Without hesitation, my daughter entered the bathroom. She didn't hesitate or say a word at first, just stepped into the shower with me, wrapping her arms around me as I stood there, broken and vulnerable. And then she whispered words that I will carry with me forever: "Like the butterfly, you are going through a metamorphosis. When this is over, you will emerge with beautiful wings and be reborn." Her words were more than comforting—they gave me hope, a belief that I could transcend this dark period and come out the other side transformed.

My son then gently shaved my head, an act of kindness that I could feel down to my bones. His hands were steady, his touch soft, and the tenderness with which he carried out this task reminded me of how deeply my children loved me. Together, they made sure my apartment was not just a place to recuperate but a space of beauty, filled with light and love.

But as much as I wanted them by my side forever, the reality was they had their own lives to return to. After a period of time, they had to leave, and I was left to face my journey alone. The next round of induction chemotherapy loomed on the horizon, and while this time I knew exactly what to expect, the knowledge didn't make it any easier.

Still, the love and strength my children had shown me gave me the courage to face the next stage. I braced myself for the isolation and the struggle that was to come, but now I understood that even in my solitude, I was never truly alone. Their support had fortified me in ways I couldn't have imagined. And though I knew the road ahead would be difficult, I was determined to face it with the same resilience they had shown me, drawing on the knowledge that, like a butterfly, I was in the midst of a transformation.

I don't think I had ever felt such a deep sense of desperation and loneliness. It was a profound isolation, unlike anything I had known before. Yet, amidst that darkness, I made a decision. I would take this time, painful as it was, to truly go within—to delve deep into the corners of my soul that had long been neglected. I would introspect, meditate, and try to listen to that quiet, aching part of me that had been crying out to be heard for so long. It was a part of me that I had ignored, drowned out by the noise of daily life and the distractions of external responsibilities.

There were countless days and nights when I found myself drowning in tears and engulfed by an overwhelming sense of solitude. Despite the care and attention I received, I often felt utterly alone, unsure if I had the strength to keep going. My sister Ginna, bless her heart, took on the responsibility of taking me to and from my hospital visits and administering my Filgrastim injections. Her visits, though brief, were a source of comfort that I cherished deeply. Yet, even with her loving presence, an undeniable loneliness persisted.

As my mind gradually settled, I found that my emotions became easier to manage. The fear and anxiety that once overwhelmed me no longer had the same grip on my heart. In their place, a realization started to dawn. I began to understand that *love*—true, unconditional love—was the highest energy, the most powerful force that could transcend any challenge. I made a conscious decision not to see my illness as a battle, but rather as a message from my body, a wise and loving attempt to alert me that something was deeply out of balance. My body wasn't betraying me; it was asking me to take notice, to pay attention to the life that was slipping through my fingers if I didn't wake up.

I realized that the love I needed to cultivate was not the self-sacrificing love I had often offered others, but a love that started within. It was the kind of love that allowed me to care for myself in a way I had never done before. To accept and honor my own needs, my own desires, my own worth. This was new territory for me, uncharted and unfamiliar. But it was also liberating. I began to understand that love could not be truly given unless it was first felt for oneself.

The physical aspect of my healing was progressing at a remarkable pace. The treatments were working, and my body was responding in ways that even the doctors described as miraculous. But the emotional and spiritual side of my healing—the deep sadness and loneliness that had been weighing on my heart—needed just as much attention. My physical recovery was only part of the story; my soul was calling out for its own kind of healing.

In that quiet space within me, I discovered a strength I hadn't known existed. It was a strength born not of resistance, but of surrender. Surrendering to the love that was always there, waiting for me to receive it.

This is where things truly became fascinating.

Miracles—or synchronicities—began to unfold one after another. It seemed that as soon as I opened myself to facing my pain and working through it, rather than resisting it, life started to flow in unexpected and magical ways.

I have always believed in the transformative power of therapy with a skilled mental health professional, so I embarked on a journey to find the right one. And then, as if guided by divine intervention, she came into my life. It felt like more than coincidence—like the work of Archangel Michael, whose energy and presence have always been a guiding force in my life. His protection and guidance led me to this therapist, and I couldn't help but feel that this connection was a gift from the angels themselves.

One morning, while having my blood drawn as part of the routine treatment, the lab technician—whom I affectionately called "my favorite vampire"—shared something that caught my attention. She spoke of a therapist she had befriended, who happened to have an office in the same building as where the lab was located. I had been searching for someone to talk to, but despite my oncologist's expertise in treating my physical illness, he hadn't been able to provide a single referral. This experience underscored a deeper issue I had noticed with Western medicine: its disconnection from treating the whole human being. While it focuses intensely on the physical body, it often neglects the mind and soul, leaving the emotional and spiritual aspects of healing largely unaddressed.

As we spoke more, my favorite vampire added, almost offhandedly, "This therapist works with angels." I was stunned. Did she just say angels? Then she elaborated, telling me how the therapist had recently returned from France and had brought back a stamp of Archangel Michael for her. I was beyond intrigued. Archangel Michael had been a powerful spiritual figure in my life since childhood, so the connection felt profound and unmistakable. I asked for the therapist's contact information, which my favorite vampire gladly shared, and that very afternoon I found myself calling her number.

When the therapist responded via WhatsApp, I immediately noticed her profile picture—it was none other than a radiant image of Archangel Michael. I couldn't believe it. This was not a coincidence. It felt like a clear, divine sign that I was exactly where I needed to be.

In June 2021, I embarked on a transformative healing journey that went far beyond the physical and mental realms—it touched my spirit. This was not just about confronting leukemia; it was about healing every part of myself. My therapist became as much of a life-saver as my oncologist. She seamlessly blended traditional psychological techniques with a deeply spiritual approach, weaving both elements together in each session. Her guidance not only helped me navigate the emotional turmoil I was facing but also reignited the spiritual teachings I had spent years exploring.

Suddenly, everything I had studied about metaphysics was unfolding in real-time within my own body, mind, and soul. The abstract concepts I had once pondered were no longer theories; they were being put to the test, and I was experiencing their truth firsthand. The intersection of science and spirituality—a fusion that has always fascinated me—was now becoming my reality. I came to realize that one cannot exist without the other. It is in this space, where the material meets the mystical, that miracles are born, where we uncover our purpose and become the heroes of our own stories.

In these moments, I discovered my true calling, my reason for being, as everything began to align. I could feel the presence of forces greater than myself guiding my path, showing me that I was never truly alone. Under the wise guidance of my therapist, I began to view leukemia through a different lens—not just as a physical ailment but as a "bloodline disorder." This illness seemed to be intricately tied to my ancestry, and that realization resonated deeply. Among my paternal grandparents' three children, each had a descendant who developed leukemia. The pattern was undeniable.

Although leukemia isn't classified as hereditary, there can be a genetic predisposition to developing it. This raised an important question: what if the roots of this illness extended beyond biology? What if the family tree itself held the key to understanding this condition? My therapist introduced me to biodecoding, a practice that seeks to uncover and heal the emotional and ancestral causes of illness. Biodecoding accesses the cellular unconscious, allowing us to revisit and resolve past traumas—both personal and inherited—that might be passed down through generations.

As I explored my family history and my own life's choices, I began to uncover the emotional weight that may have contributed to my illness. The belief that leukemia could carry emotional and psychological weight from our lineage—that unresolved traumas were silently waiting to be acknowledged—profoundly shifted my approach to healing. This process wasn't just about treating the disease but about unraveling my family's emotional history and healing those wounds at their deepest level.

The more I learned, the more I realized that true healing involves understanding all dimensions of the human experience. One book that deeply resonated with me was *Cured* by Dr. Jeffrey Rediger. He, like many progressive physicians, embraced integrative healing methods and emphasized the importance of not just physical nutrition, but also emotional well-being—how we think, feel, and connect with others. What we believe, he argued, is just as crucial to our healing.

CHAPTER 2

*"So, what do we know about healing beyond
physical treatment? Beyond our body, our soul and
our feelings play an important role in healing."*

- Bert Hellinger, founder of Family Constellations

To move forward, we often must look back. This principle guided me on my transformative journey of biodecoding, where I traced the intricate threads of my ancestral lineage and revisited my family's story. I delved deep into the past, seeking clues and uncovering patterns woven through generations, each shedding light on why certain afflictions had repeatedly surfaced within our family tree.

It became clear that the past held the key—not only to understanding the roots of my illness but also to unraveling the choices I had made throughout my life, which led me to this pivotal moment and the challenges I faced. What began as a quest for healing evolved into a profound reflection on my existence. Each memory and fragment of my family history turned into lessons waiting to be discovered, puzzles yearning to be solved.

With the methodical curiosity I had honed as a teacher, I sought to extract meaning from the experiences that shaped me. In this memoir, I invite you to join me as I share the insights and revelations from my journey—one that illuminated the interconnectedness of our stories and the healing power within them.

On July 17, 2021, a single word stood out from my lab results: REMISSION. This was not just a medical victory but an invitation to embrace a new chapter of self-discovery and purpose.

It also signaled an opportunity to serve others in the only meaningful way I knew how—through teaching. A unique offer came my way: an invitation to tutor two sets of siblings in the breathtaking surroundings of Lake Atitlán, Guatemala, specifically in the remote and tranquil area of Xepotrela, nestled in San Pablo la Laguna.

Xepotrela had recently become home to a community of passionate energy healers who had founded a center called "Sante," meaning "health" in French. This center, situated in the heart of the mountains, radiated a sense of purpose and healing. I accepted the tutoring position, eager to support the educational needs of the founders' children. Living high in the mountains surrounding this healing sanctuary, I was immersed in an environment unlike any I had experienced before.

The energy of Xepotrela was palpable, emanating from the ancient rocks that had been revered by the indigenous community for generations. Natural caves and towering stone formations served as sites for sacred ceremonies, channels for a deep, primal healing energy that pulsed through the Earth itself. In this awe-inspiring setting, I realized that teaching these children was not merely an educational endeavor—it was an opportunity to contribute to a broader journey of healing and growth, both for myself and those around me.

In this sacred environment, I came to a profound realization—I had been spared. I had been granted precious time on this Earth because my soul still had a purpose to fulfill. Here, I embraced a new mantra: "ASK. BELIEVE.

LET IT HAPPEN. SAY THANK YOU." With this, I sent my intentions out into the Universe, trusting that it would respond. My focus shifted from escape to healing, from evasion to acceptance, and I surrendered myself to the magic of Lake Atitlán, letting its majestic beauty envelop me, offering solace and strength.

As I ascended the hundred or so stairs to my room at Sante, I was greeted by a view that left me breathless. Before me stretched the most awe-inspiring panorama of the lake I had ever encountered. Until that moment, I thought the view from Santa Catarina Palopó was unmatched, but this vista was something else entirely. From my vantage point, I could see the full expanse of volcanoes, their peaks rising majestically above the lake's shimmering surface. On clear days, I could even catch a glimpse of the active Fuego Volcano, its fiery presence adding to the lake's mystical allure.

Every morning, I awoke to this stunning spectacle, witnessing breathtaking sunrises and sunsets that unfolded like a vivid tapestry. The lake, with its vibrant energy, cradled me in a safe and nurturing embrace. In this sacred space, I found profound peace. I could sleep, rest, teach, and simply *be*. The love and protection I felt from nature moved me to tears of joy and gratitude for the beauty, healing, and gift of life I had been given. The lake, the mountains, and the vibrant energy of Xepotrela became my sanctuary—a place where I could reconnect with my soul and purpose, enveloped in nature's immense love and power.

It was in this extraordinary setting that I began to write this story.

"San Pablo la Laguna, Lake Atitlan, Solola, Guatemala"

CHAPTER 3

*"Through being born into a family, we inherit
not only our biological genes, but also our
belief systems and behavior patterns."*

– Joy Manne, PhD

The Martini surname has its origins in Genoa, Italy. However, the details of how this surname came to settle in Central America - to this day remain something of a mystery. One popular family rumor suggests that my great-grandfather arrived in America like many immigrants of his time, passing through Ellis Island before making his way to the West Coast, residing in San Francisco for a while and then traveling south to eventually settle in Central America. Another, perhaps more plausible, theory is that he ventured to Central America to work on the construction of the Panama Canal. It was there, in the melting pot of workers from around the world, that he allegedly met my great-grandmother, a native of Honduras. How exactly they found their way to Quetzaltenango, Guatemala, remains unclear, but it was there that my grandfather, Miguel Angel Martini Salinas, was born.

My grandfather, the youngest of 13 children, entered the world when his parents were already well into their later years. Tragically, he became an orphan by the age of eight, left in the care of his eldest siblings, Sofia and Juan. Miguel Angel's life took a pivotal turn at 13 when he was sent to the capital city of Guatemala to attend boarding school in pursuit of a better education.

By the age of 16, he had completed his secondary studies, proving himself to be both intellectually gifted and socially adept. His knack for numbers and natural charm made him a standout, much like his father, whose adventurous spirit had led him to leave Italy and journey to the Americas. Miguel Angel followed in those footsteps, becoming a traveling salesman at a time when such a profession held both promise and danger. The early 1900s were not known for infrastructure in this underdeveloped country—many of the areas he ventured to were accessible only by horse, donkey, or makeshift vehicles that had to navigate rugged, unpaved roads.

This life on the road, full of both risk and reward, shaped him into the kind of man who was admired by many. Handsome, intelligent, hardworking, and full of the zest for life, my grandfather embodied the Martini spirit of adventure and perseverance. He was undoubtedly seen as quite the "catch," admired not only for his good looks and charm but for his honesty and unwavering dedication to his work. His story, like that of our family, is one of resilience, of seeking opportunity in new and unfamiliar lands, and of building a legacy that would ripple through generations.

As a traveling salesman, Miguel Angel frequently found himself visiting the central customs office, where a young woman named Olga, my grandmother, worked. What made Olga stand out wasn't just the fact that she was a woman, but that she was the only woman in an environment dominated by men. Despite the progressive air of the "Roaring '20s," Guatemala remained a conservative society, and it was unusual, even frowned upon, for a woman of her status to be working at all, let alone in a bustling, testosterone-fueled customs office.

Yet, Olga was grateful for the opportunity. As the eldest of four siblings, she had taken on the responsibility of supporting her family after the sudden death of their father, Enrique Padilla, who had tragically passed away from a heart attack at the super young age of 33. His untimely death left his wife, Betzabe, a young widow with four children: Olga, Marta, Laura, and Oscar.

Betzabe, my great grandmother, like many women of her social standing, had little formal education. She was a member of the middle-class whose life had been largely centered around domestic duties. Her hands were skilled in sewing, though she wasn't a professional seamstress. She managed to bring in a modest income by altering and creating garments for friends and family. However, it was far from enough to sustain her family.

Seeing the need, Olga took the initiative to find work. With her primary education complete and a talent for typing, she secured a position through a family connection at the "Aduana Central," the central customs office of Guatemala. This job was not just a necessity; it was a lifeline for her family.

But Olga was more than just a competent worker. Her looks were matched by an appealing personality that set her apart in the office. She was diligent and responsible, excelling in her duties. At the same time, she possessed a quirky sense of humor and a natural ability to read people, traits that earned her the admiration of her colleagues. In this male-dominated world, Olga learned to navigate the culture with grace and confidence. She even adopted some of their habits, like smoking a pipe, and could hold her own in the banter and gossip that flowed through the office. Yet, she never lost her ladylike composure, a quality that garnered her respect and admiration from everyone around her.

Olga's presence in that office wasn't just a reflection of her personal strength—it was a testament to her unwavering determination to support her family and thrive in a world that wasn't always welcoming to women in her position.

Miguel Angel couldn't help but notice Olga's charm and resilience. Before long, they became a couple. Their courtship stretched over five years, during which Miguel Angel hesitated to fully commit. As a traveling salesman, he was constantly on the road, enjoying the freedom and excitement of bachelorhood. However, Olga, approaching her 23rd birthday, was well aware of societal pressures. In those days, remaining unmarried past a certain age could brand a woman as an "old maid." Determined not to let that happen, she put her foot down and gave Miguel Angel an ultimatum.

Her bold move worked. Within the year—1935—they were married. By the following year, Olga was pregnant with their first child, a son. On February 27, 1936, Miguel Angel Martini Padilla was born, the first of three children and, as fate would have it, my father.

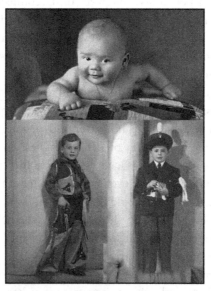

"My father, Miguel Angel Martini Padilla"

Olga and Miguel Angel were dedicated parents who ensured their children had the best of everything. They poured their time, energy, and resources into providing a stable and comfortable life, one befitting their middle-class status. Their children attended private schools and lived in a beautiful home in the heart of Guatemala City. Their residence in Zone 1 was conveniently located near the city's historic landmarks, including the Central Park, the National Palace, the Main Cathedral, and the elegant Portal del Comercio, where the finest goods from across the globe could be found.

Young Miguel, their firstborn, was blessed not only with striking good looks but also with a sharp intellect. He excelled in his academic pursuits, quickly distinguishing himself as a bright student. He attended "Colegio La Preparatoria," or "La Prepa," a prestigious private boys' school where families of a certain social standing sent their sons for a top-tier, secular education. Although both Olga and Miguel Angel were devout Catholics, they recognized the potential pitfalls of an overly religious education and wanted their children to learn in an environment that encouraged independent thinking.

In this nurturing atmosphere, their children thrived, enjoying the privileges and opportunities afforded to them by their parents' dedication and foresight. Life for Olga, Miguel Angel, and their family seemed to follow a script of stability, success, and comfort—a testament to the choices and sacrifices that had brought them to this point.

Young Miguel not only excelled academically but also possessed a magnetic personality that charmed everyone around him. His charisma captured the attention of many young girls and even the admiration of the women who owned and ran the prestigious school he attended. These two sisters had dedicated their lives to providing a world-class education for the future leaders of the country, and they saw great potential in Miguel.

His academic achievements were unparalleled; he was an A+ honors student, always at the top of his class.

In addition to his academic prowess, Miguel had a passion for basketball, which set him apart from his peers. Guatemala's national sport is fútbol (soccer), and every boy grows up playing it. Fútbol is seen as the quintessential masculine sport, while basketball, with its shorter, tighter shorts (at the time), didn't hold the same appeal or cultural significance. Miguel's father was initially hesitant about his son's choice of sport. It wasn't considered "manly" enough. However, as he had done with all of his son's endeavors, he eventually gave in, recognizing that his boy's interests mattered, even if they diverged from tradition.

Upon graduating from "La Prepa" with the highest honors, Miguel faced a bright future. His academic brilliance and dedication had earned him accolades, and his teachers encouraged him to pursue a career in medicine. They saw in him the potential to become a doctor—something rare in his lineage. Coming from a family of hardworking but non-professional men, Miguel's decision to study medicine was a bold and pioneering move. He would become the first in his family to pursue a doctorate degree, breaking away from the traditional path and forging a new legacy.

Miguel's ambition to enter the medical field was fueled not only by his intellect but also by his desire to contribute something greater to the world. The encouragement of his mentors, combined with his determination, set him on a course that would shape his future and distinguish him as a maverick in his family's history. This path of higher education and professional ambition marked a significant shift, both for Miguel personally and for the legacy of the Martini family.

In another part of Guatemala City, far from the bustling center where the elite resided, there stood a grand estate known as "Villa Zoila." This magnificent villa, located in Zone 10 of the city, was built by a man of considerable influence and wealth, Victor Lainfiesta Dorion, my maternal grandfather, as a tribute to his second consort, Zoila Castellanos, my grandmother. The estate's location on the outskirts of the city was no accident. Victor was a powerful figure, closely tied to one of the most prominent leaders of the time—General Jorge Ubico, the man who ruled Guatemala from 1931 to 1944.

Victor's sister, Marta Lainfiesta Dorion, was married to Ubico, who was often referred to as "Central America's Napoleon" for his military prowess and authoritative rule. Ubico rose to power in 1931, assuming the presidency in what was more of a symbolic election. His reign, lasting from 1931 to 1944, was one of dictatorship rather than democracy, but like many authoritarian leaders, his legacy was complex. He was responsible for several progressive reforms and long-lasting institutions that shaped Guatemala, even as his regime enforced strict control and often suppressed opposition.

If judged by today's standards, Ubico would be labeled a despot military dictator, an authoritarian who often used brutal methods. But during his time he also had quite a few accomplishments, especially as the world was engulfed in the chaos of World War II, his leadership provided a degree of stability and development that was rare, restoring international credit, building roads and public works, improving public health and eliminating corruption. In fact, he left Guatemala's treasury in better shape than he found it, something no Guatemalan leader - ever since - has managed. Yet, he had a grand sense of self-importance. Known for his dashing good looks, he often paraded through the streets of the city on a white horse, styled in the image of Napoleon himself. His flair for extravagance only deepened his mythos, and his appearances were always marked by pomp and spectacle.

Marta, Ubico's wife and my grandfather's sister, came from a noble and affluent background, yet her role was mostly one of decorum and social standing. Like many women of her era, she was not seen as an equal partner in her marriage, and their union was childless, fueling rumors about Ubico's infertility. Some whispered that a war injury had left him unable to father children.

Victor, on the other hand, was a man of the land. Despite his wealth and stature, he saw himself as a farmer, overseeing vast estates and spending much of his time hunting—a popular pastime among men of his class. By all accounts, Victor was a fair and just landowner, known for treating his workers with dignity and compassion. Yet, he was also a product of his time, a charismatic and influential figure whose relationship with Ubico brought him into the highest circles of power. Together, the two men were a common sight in Guatemala City, sometimes even riding their matching motorcycles through the streets, embodying the privilege and authority they wielded.

Victor Lainfiesta Dorion was married to a woman of equal social standing from the prominent Farnes family. Together, they had six children, the Lainfiesta Farnes. On the surface, their marriage seemed to reflect the typical union of two families from Guatemala's upper echelon, respected and wealthy. However, Victor's life took an unexpected turn during one of the many grand parades he would attend with his brother-in-law, General Jorge Ubico. As the two men rode through the streets in their characteristic display of power and prestige, Victor's eyes fell upon a woman in the crowd who would change his life forever.

Her name was Zoila Castellanos de Valdez. Zoila was a married woman with four children—Amparo, Gloria, Eduardo, and Violeta—whose ages ranged from 15 to 5. Despite their respective family obligations, an undeniable attraction developed between Victor and Zoila, leaving

Victor torn between his duties as a family man and the deep, unexpected love he felt for Zoila.

At that time, Guatemala's rigid societal structure, guided by strict Catholic values, made divorce illegal and socially unacceptable. Both the Church and high society condemned the mere notion of dissolving a marriage, making Victor's dilemma not only a personal crisis but also a potential social catastrophe. What were Victor and Zoila to do? The consequences of their decision would reverberate far beyond their immediate families.

In a bold and controversial move, both Victor and Zoila left their respective spouses, a decision that sent shockwaves through their social circles. Zoila brought her four children with her, but Victor made the heartbreaking decision to leave his six children behind. The scandal that followed was monumental. To escape the scrutiny and judgment of the public, Victor built an opulent villa on the outskirts of Guatemala City, Villa Zoila, where he and Zoila could live together with her children.

Their union, though mired in controversy, flourished in its own way. Victor and Zoila went on to have two daughters of their own, Blanca Luz and 5 years later their youngest, Myriam Stella—my mother. Despite the scandal and the societal condemnation that followed them, they built a life together, one marked by love, defiance, and the creation of a new family against the odds.

"My mother, Myriam Stella Lainfiesta Castellanos"

I can only imagine the surprise and perhaps shock that Myriam's arrival must have brought to both Victor and Zoila. By the time she was born, they were already quite advanced in years—Victor in his 60s and Zoila in her 40s. Myriam's birth was nothing short of a miracle of nature, considering the age of her parents. She grew into a vibrant, healthy, and beautiful woman, despite the societal shame, judgment, and guilt that surrounded her birth out of wedlock. Her existence carried a mark of scandal, yet she thrived, proving that life can flourish even in the most challenging circumstances.

Victor adored his youngest daughter Myriam; she became the light of his life. However, Zoila, perhaps exhausted from years of raising children, seemed less enamored. By the time

Myriam arrived, it's possible Zoila had grown weary of the duties of motherhood. But whatever the case, Myriam was an extraordinary child. From the moment she was born, her beauty captivated everyone around her—blonde hair, flawless fair skin, and striking greenish-honey eyes that sparkled with life. By the age of 14, she was already winning beauty contests, and at 17, she took home the crown of "La Reina del Café," one of the most prestigious titles in the country.

Despite her beauty and charm, Myriam's education didn't seem to be a priority for her family. Most of her time was spent on the family's farms, where she thrived in the natural surroundings. She loved the freedom of the countryside, climbing trees and mingling with the farm laborers and their families. Myriam had a deep affinity for animals, constantly rescuing and nurturing them. She became known for her love of dogs, caring for hundreds of them well into her later years.

Though she preferred the tomboyish life of scraped knees and wild adventures in the countryside, Myriam was still expected to uphold the family name. She was, after all, a Lainfiesta, and no matter the stain of her parents' unconventional relationship, she was raised to be a lady. When in the city, she was expected to attend school and behave in accordance with the high standards of Guatemalan society.

When Myriam was a young teenager, her sister, Blanca Luz, got married and moved to New Orleans. Myriam was then sent to help her sister care for her children, the first two of what eventually would be seven in all, and this turned out to be a fortunate event for Myriam. Living in the United States, she quickly picked up English while she befriended many of her new neighbors. Upon returning to Guatemala, fluent in English, Myriam became quite the star at the prestigious English American School. Her new language skills, combined with her beauty, made her incredibly popular, and it was no surprise when she was crowned prom queen.

Myriam was not just blessed with beauty; she possessed a natural wisdom and a deep sense of compassion. Her love for animals was evident from an early age, and naturally, she dreamed of becoming a veterinarian. But when she shared this ambition with her father, Victor, his response was firm: "No, that's a man's job." Victor held traditional views about what was appropriate for women, and becoming a vet did not fit his ideals.

Undeterred, Myriam proposed a different path—she could become a teacher. She had always found joy in helping the children of the farm laborers, teaching them to read and write. However, this idea met the same fate as the first. Victor dismissed it with a wave, declaring, "Teachers are communists."

Still not willing to give up, Myriam considered nursing, a profession that aligned perfectly with her nurturing nature and desire to help others. But again, Victor shut down her aspirations. "Nurses are loose women," he insisted, his words reflecting the rigid gender roles of his time.

Despite these constant rejections, Myriam never lost sight of her passion to care for others. Years passed, and life unfolded, but her dream of becoming a nurse lingered in her heart. In an extraordinary twist of fate, when most people are thinking about retirement, Myriam finally fulfilled that dream. At the age of 65, she pursued a nursing degree, proving that it is never too late to follow your calling. Against the odds, she graduated, stepping into a profession that had long been denied to her. Her resilience and determination showed that no matter the age, passion and purpose can be realized.

Whereas, Victor viewed most professions as unsuitable for a woman of Myriam's social standing. In his mind, the only acceptable career outside the home for a lady was that of a secretary. And with Myriam's ability to speak English, the role of a "Bilingual Secretary" seemed to him a perfect fit.

While attending the English American School, Myriam

befriended a classmate named Olga Leticia Martini, the sister of a certain young man who would soon change her life—Miguel Angel Martini. Handsome, intelligent, and charming, Miguel quickly caught Myriam's attention. Their courtship began when Myriam was just 15 years old, while Miguel was already studying medicine at the prestigious "Real y Pontificia Universidad de San Carlos Borromeo", an institution dating back to Guatemala's colonial era in the late 1600s. Meanwhile, Myriam was set to transfer to the Colegio Belga de Guatemala to pursue secretarial studies, a path she did not enjoy.

"Mom & Dad"

Unlike Miguel, who thrived in medical school, Myriam found herself miserable at secretary school. Typing and shorthand felt like a chore, and she detested the work. Yet, she knew she had to graduate, and soon, as she was pregnant and had to prepare for marriage.

According to family lore, Myriam's parents were unaware of her pregnancy when they agreed to let her marry Miguel. They imposed one condition: she had to finish her secretarial degree first. This arrangement seems curious, given how much Victor and Zoila valued appearances and societal expectations. Would they truly allow their daughter to marry a penniless medical student with an uncertain future? Perhaps they saw potential in Miguel's future as a doctor, or maybe they were simply exhausted by parenthood by that stage and eager to see their youngest daughter settled.

Whatever their reasons, Myriam and Miguel were married on February 16, 1958. A few months later, on July 5, 1958, they welcomed their first child—me.

Being the first grandchild on my father's side was a momentous occasion. Olga and Miguel Ángel were absolutely overjoyed at my arrival, as their eldest son had just made them grandparents. On my mother's side, however, the excitement was more subdued. Victor, my grandfather, was the only one who seemed genuinely pleased with his baby girl becoming a mother herself.

Sadly, when I was just six months old, Victor suffered a debilitating stroke that left him paralyzed on his right side. He passed away three months later. But before his death, a quick and carefully planned marital arrangement was put into motion to ensure his affairs were in order. Victor signed all the necessary legal documents, leaving Zoila, now as his second wife, with control over his estate. It was now up to her to distribute the inheritance between her daughters, Blanca Luz and Myriam, as well as Victor's children from his first marriage, and even Zoila's children from her previous marriage, for whom Victor had become a stepfather.

Zoila, a shrewd and calculating woman, ensured that her

own children from her previous marriage were well provided for. Although my mother and her sister Blanca Luz received an inheritance as well after their father's passing, that inheritance dwindled over time, largely benefiting Zoila's children.

By the time I was born, my father was still in medical school, and their only income came from a side job he had selling cars at the new Ford Motor Company agency, where my grandfather had recently started working after years as a traveling salesman. During this period, my parents lived with my paternal grandparents and my aunt Thelma, who was only 11 years old at the time. Determined to secure a sense of independence, my mother used her inheritance to buy a home of her own—a significant step that included the luxury of a television, which was rare in those days. This house was intended to be a fresh start for my parents, a chance to build their life together despite the challenges of a young family and uncertain financial future.

However, my mother's hopes were soon dashed. The house quickly became a home to everyone, and instead of assuming the role of its lady, she was treated more as a daughter than the woman of her own household. My grandmother Olga, assertive and commanding, took control, managing the household and making most of the decisions. My mother's voice was scarcely heard, even in matters related to raising me.

When I was four years old, my mother became pregnant with my brother, and that same year my father graduated from medical school. In a gesture that meant the world to me, my father dedicated his thesis to me—a symbol of his deep love and pride.

CHAPTER 4

"I love walking in nature, and it is for me a kind of religion. There is no need to run to a temple, every breath, every step in nature can be a place of worship."

– Thich Nhat Hanh

The future was bright for my father. He quickly made an impression, dazzling his mentors and professors with his skill and intellect. Deciding to pursue the highest specialty in medicine, he set his sights on becoming a surgeon. His extraordinary talent didn't go unnoticed—he possessed what people called "magical hands," capable of performing the most delicate and intricate surgical procedures. One of his professors was so impressed that he sent an application on my father's behalf to the prestigious Leighey Clinic in Boston, Massachusetts. To everyone's delight, my father was accepted, securing a place to specialize in thoracic surgery and setting the stage for what promised to be an extraordinary career.

Moving to Boston marked a significant change for our family, but for me, it came during a time of quiet recovery. At just five years old, I had been diagnosed with hepatitis A. The illness slowed me down, forcing me to embrace stillness and introspection far earlier than most people. My recovery required calm and solitude, and during those long, quiet hours,

I began to sense that life extended beyond the physical. Even then, I intuitively felt there was something deeper, an unseen force that connected everything.

Much of my healing took place outdoors, basking in the sunlight, surrounded by nature's beauty in Guatemala, the "Land of Eternal Spring." The vibrant colors of flowers, the rustling of trees, the lush green grass, and the constant presence of Nube, my white bunny, filled my days with quiet wonder. Nature became my refuge, awakening my senses and deepening my awareness. Even as a young child, I felt a sacred connection to the natural world—its rhythms, its grace, its silent wisdom. It was as though nature itself whispered truths to me, offering solace and understanding in ways that words could not.

This connection to the natural world, with its vast beauty and quiet power, never left me. It would follow me to other places, like Lake Atitlán, whose majestic energy would later touch my soul with the same profound reverence I felt in that backyard as a child.

At my maternal grandmother's country villa, "San Miguel," another piece of my spiritual journey took root. A copper statue of Archangel Michael, standing guard in the garden, captivated me. His fierce armor and gleaming sword, paired with his divine wings, stirred something deep within. Though I couldn't fully comprehend it at the time, Archangel Michael became a spiritual companion, a guiding force I would grow to understand more intimately throughout my life. His presence, both protective and transcendent, resonated with my young mind, awakening a sense of divine connection that would shape my spiritual path.

Though I couldn't articulate it as a child, this early knowledge planted the seed for a lifelong search for deeper meaning. As I grew, I immersed myself in reading, exploring religious traditions, and studying philosophies, all of which led to a profound realization: we are not just physical beings with souls, but souls experiencing life through the body. This understanding deepened over time, guiding me to see that our souls are part of a larger, interconnected divine whole, woven into the fabric of the universe.

At 62, when I was diagnosed with acute myeloid leukemia (AML), I had already lived a life full of joy, pain, and reflection. The years of spiritual inquiry had prepared me for this profound challenge. Rather than viewing my illness as a punishment, I saw it as "The Ultimate Teacher," an opportunity for transformation. The vulnerability and isolation that came with it opened me in ways I had never before experienced, teaching me the true meaning of healing—not just of the body, but of the soul.

True healing, I realized, was not about erasing the difficult parts of life, but about embracing all of it. It meant looking at the past and the present with clarity, without judgment or blame. Healing was about accepting life's pain and beauty with equal grace, finding meaning in every experience. This understanding became my guide, reminding me that healing is not about fixing what is broken, but about opening ourselves fully to life—with compassion, objectivity, and a sense of divine purpose.

As I was recovering from hepatitis, or perhaps shortly after, preparations for my father's journey to Boston began. He left ahead of us to begin his medical training and secure a place for us to live once we joined him. Meanwhile, life at home became consumed with a different set of preparations—those for my First Communion. My grandparents, devout Catholics, believed it was important for me to receive the sacrament before we left Guatemala, even though I had just turned six.

The entire household was buzzing with activity, each member assigned a specific role for this milestone event in my young life. My great-grandmother Betzabé, my grandmother

Olga's mother, was living with us at the time and she took on the responsibility of teaching me the prayers. Despite her age, she still possessed remarkable dexterity, she sewed my First Communion dress and veil. Spending time with her was always a joy. She was patient, kind, and always smelled wonderful—a comforting presence. As she guided me through prayers, she also passed down her knowledge of sewing, a skill I still cherish today. Although I prefer picking up a crochet hook instead of a sewing needle, in both activities the main ingredient is the same - patience.

My mother, determined to add her own touch to the celebration, enrolled in a pastry class to learn how to make the cake decorations. I vividly remember accompanying her to the neighbor's house where she took her lessons. The intricate flowers she crafted out of icing were so delicate and beautiful that it seemed almost impossible they were meant to be eaten. I regret that we have no photographs of that magnificent cake.

As the big day approached, my grandparents presented me with a treasured gift: a small prayer book with mother-of-pearl covers, a golden crucifix adorning the front, a gold latch, and pages edged in gold. It became my most prized possession, something I cherished for years. The day itself promised to be a grand event. There would be a piñata, party favors, and special milk-and-cinnamon candies made by the nuns. My grandmother Olga's famous tamales were to be served, and all of our extended family had been invited. I was filled with excitement.

"My First Communion (6 years old)"

However, amid all the excitement, no one had mentioned a crucial detail: in order to take my First Communion, I first had to go through the sacrament of Confession. At just six years old, the very idea of Confession terrified me. I couldn't grasp the notion of entering a dark confessional booth, kneeling down, and confessing my "sins" to a faceless priest hidden behind a partition. Even more baffling to my young mind was the concept of sin itself. My great-grandmother Betzabé had taught me the Ten Commandments, and I understood that breaking them was considered sinful, but I genuinely couldn't think of anything I had done that violated those rules.

As the moment of Confession drew nearer, panic set in. I had to think of something to say, and quickly. My mind raced until, trembling with nerves, I came up with a small fabrication. I invented a story about hiding my mother's keys to make her worry—an imaginary act of mischief that, in my young mind, would surely qualify as a sin. I entered the confessional, knees shaking, and told my fabricated tale. To my relief, the priest listened and then assigned me the standard penance: a few Hail Marys and an Our Father. And just like that, my "sin" was absolved.

So, there it was—my first act of contrition, based on a lie I made up out of fear, all so that I could receive the body of Christ for the first time. Even at six years old, I knew something was off about the whole experience.

After the sacred sacrament of my First Communion was complete, the focus quickly shifted to preparations for our journey to Boston to reunite with my father. The excitement of travel filled the air, though my memories of Boston itself are faint. What stands out most vividly is our small apartment, where we spent the majority of our time during those early months in a foreign land. I was too young to fully grasp the significance of why we were there, but in hindsight, that period marked a major turning point in my father's medical career and our family's destiny.

As my father completed his residency in thoracic surgery, his exceptional talent began to attract attention. One person in particular who noticed his skill was a highly respected pediatric surgeon at Montreal's Children's Hospital in Canada. He was impressed by my father's meticulous and precise approach in the operating room, recognizing in him the potential to become an outstanding pediatric surgeon.

Seeing promise in this young doctor, he extended a personal invitation for him to join the residency program at Montreal Children's Hospital. This opportunity was too significant to pass up, and my father eagerly accepted. Thus, in 1965, we packed up once again and moved—this time to Montreal, Canada, a new chapter in our lives beginning in another foreign land, full of promise for my father's career and a world of unknowns for the rest of us.

CHAPTER 5

*"Then there was the pain. A breaking and entering
when even the senses are torn apart. The act of
rape on an eight-year-old body is a matter of
the needle giving because the camel can't."*

- Maya Angelou, "I Know Why the Caged Bird Sings"

Montreal quickly became my favorite place of all the places we eventually lived in. Even though I was quite young, I could still appreciate the richness of its culture, the beauty of the architecture, the immaculate streets, and most of all, the warmth of the people. It had a unique charm that left a lasting impression on me.

I was enrolled at St. Paul's Academy for girls, a school run by nuns—though I can't recall their specific order. I have very fond memories of my time there, as it was where I truly mastered the English language and where I was exposed to the love for reading. My brother, on the other hand, attended St. Leon's School for boys, which was operated by priests who spoke primarily French. He was just three years old at the time but picked up the language quickly. However, with Spanish spoken at home, English all around him, and French at school, he created a hybrid language that only we seemed to understand. It was an amusing mix of all three languages, and while it made perfect sense to us, outsiders had a bit more trouble deciphering his unique way of speaking.

As children, my brother and I thrived in Montreal. We enjoyed our schools, and the people we encountered were always kind and gentle. Even the crossing guards, who were part of the Mounted Police, were cheerful and attentive, making our daily routines feel safe and enjoyable. But while we adapted easily to life in Montreal, things were not as simple for our parents.

My father was excelling in his residency, making strides in his medical career, but the modest salary of a resident wasn't enough to support a family of four. The financial pressure became a concern, and my mother realized she had to step in and contribute. Dusting off the secretarial skills she had learned back in Guatemala, she began looking for work.

Fortuitously, there was an opening for an operating room (OR) secretary at the same hospital where my father was training. Mrs. Murphy, the head of the secretarial pool, was immediately charmed by my mother's warm, friendly demeanor and hired her to transcribe the surgeons' recorded notes after each procedure. Since the Montreal Children's Hospital was a teaching institution, every operation was recorded for educational purposes, and my mother was tasked with converting these recordings into patient records.

My mother flourished in her new role. For the first time in her life, she was doing something outside the confines of being an obedient daughter, a wife, or a mother. She was working, interacting with doctors, nurses, and administrative staff, and she quickly became well-liked by everyone around her. Her income soon surpassed my father's, making her the primary breadwinner of the family.

Despite my mother's new job and the income she brought in, the money still wasn't enough to sustain us. As a result, my brother and I were sent back to Guatemala to live with our paternal grandparents. It seemed that while my father continued his residency at the Montreal Children's Hospital, they couldn't afford to keep us all together in Canada. But instead of leaving us with our mother, it was decided that we would return to Guatemala, as my father needed her by his side more than ever.

He was the one with the needs, the one whose demands always took priority. He required constant attention, emotional support, and, in a sense, mothering. My mom, in turn, had to fulfill that role, putting aside her own needs and even those of her children. It became clear that when a husband demands such nurturing energy from his partner, almost in an infantile way, the children inevitably bear the cost.

This dynamic wasn't new. It had happened before. Before my father had been invited to do his surgical residency in Boston, he had been named Director of a rural hospital in Cobán, a remote region of Guatemala. Even though my brother was not yet one year old, my mom was summoned to join him there. She was put on a bus and sent to the isolated town to tend to my father's emotional needs, leaving my baby brother and me behind with our grandparents. He had been too lonely, too helpless to endure the separation from her, even at the expense of her being away from us.

And so, in 1967, history repeated itself. My brother and I were sent back to Guatemala, leaving my parents to navigate life together in Montreal while we were left in the familiar yet distant care of our grandparents. It was a pattern, one where my father's needs took precedence, and we were often pushed into the background of his life's story.

The Mayan School, a private bilingual institution in Guatemala City, was where my parents—or perhaps it was my grandparents—decided I should attend. Their goal was to ensure I wouldn't lose my recently acquired English skills. It was 1967, and Guatemala's political climate was tense. Julio

César Méndez Montenegro was the president, the first civilian to hold that office after a long line of military rulers. The civil war had just ignited, with the early signs of terrorism already rippling through the country. This brutal conflict would go on for the next 36 years, leaving more than 200,000 people dead or disappeared, most of them of Mayan descent. The driving force behind it all was the fear of communism. The United States, heavily involved, was later implicated in numerous human rights violations, with their training of Guatemalan officers in counterinsurgency tactics.

In this turbulent atmosphere, a private American school bearing the name "Mayan School" was an easy target for attacks, a bitter irony given the indigenous population's suffering during this time. One morning, during class, we were suddenly instructed to hide beneath our desks. The loud, popping sounds of gunfire echoed outside, mingling with the acrid smell of smoke and gunpowder that began to seep into our classroom. We didn't fully understand what was happening, but the tension in the air was palpable. The fear in the faces of our teachers and the strange silence that had fallen over us filled our young bodies with dread.

Suddenly, a figure burst into the room. Our teacher shouted for him to stop, demanding he identify himself, but the man moved quickly, his footsteps firm and purposeful as he ignored her commands. He knelt down under each desk, looking intently for someone. When he reached mine, he swept me into his strong arms. It was my grandfather—my rescuer. He had heard the news of the gunfight on the radio and had come to save me from whatever horrors were unfolding just beyond the school's walls.

As he ran through the school, he shielded my eyes with his coat, but I caught a glimpse of the chaos. My school bus, the one I rode every day, was in sight. Lying next to it was the bus driver, a man who had always been kind to me. He was sprawled out on the ground in a way that seemed unnatural, surrounded by a pool of red. Though I was too young to fully comprehend what I was seeing, the sense of fear and panic in the air made it clear that something terrible had happened.

During the car ride home, I don't recall speaking a word. My grandfather drove in silence, his face tense with worry. When we arrived at the house, my grandmother met us at the door with a warm cup of tea. I could hear them whispering urgently, trying to maintain a sense of calm around me, but I could tell that things were far from normal. Something terrible had happened, and though they tried to protect me from the gravity of it, I could feel the weight of the danger that had briefly entered my life.

Soon after, we found ourselves back in Montreal. I don't clearly recall whether our parents came to retrieve us or if our grandparents accompanied us on the journey back, but what remains vivid in my memory is that we arrived just in time for one of the most unforgettable events of my childhood—Expo '67, officially known as the 1967 International and Universal Exposition.

"Mom, Dad, my brother and me at Expo '67, Montreal, Canada"

The grandeur and spectacle of that event left an indelible mark on me. It was unlike anything I had ever seen before. The Expo grounds were set up on an artificial island on the St. Lawrence River, with pavilions spread across the picturesque St. Helen's Island. Even now, some remnants of the Expo remain, like the iconic geodesic dome that housed futuristic exhibits, complete with a monorail that zipped through it. One of my clearest memories was riding that monorail with my grandfather, marveling at a demonstration of long-distance communication. In this exhibit, two Japanese children were portraied in a living room somewhere in America talking in real-time through a TV screen with their grandparents in Japan—and they could actually see them! My grandfather found the whole concept too far-fetched to be believable. I wonder what he would think now, in a world where virtual meetings and video calls have become an everyday reality.

Expo '67 was an event that sparked something deep within me. From the moment we received our Expo "passports," I was utterly captivated. The concept was brilliant—you needed to get your passport stamped at each pavilion, as if you were truly visiting a different country. It was a magical experience. Among my favorite pavilions were the U.S.S.R. pavilion, where a massive glass water tank filled with Sturgeon—the fish that produced their famed caviar—greeted visitors at the entrance, and the Thailand pavilion, which seemed to shimmer as though made entirely of gold. Shaped like a giant ornate canoe, the pavilion offered a glimpse into a world filled with breathtaking beauty. Inside, I was awestruck by the intricate statues and figurines that adorned the space.

It was in that golden pavilion that I first encountered a statue of Buddha. His peaceful, serene posture drew me in, and even as a young child, I felt an immediate connection. There was something otherworldly about the calm that radiated from him, a sense of quiet power and tranquility that stayed with me long after I left the pavilion. That initial meeting with Buddha ignited a curiosity within me, a yearning to understand the deeper meaning behind the calm he exuded—a curiosity that would continue to grow and that I would continue to explore throughout my life.

Returning to the serene beauty of cultured Montreal was not the joyful homecoming I had hoped for. The peace of my childhood was shattered the day Tito stepped into our apartment, bringing with him an ominous darkness that forever marked the end of my innocence. Tito, a twisted and dangerous young man in his twenties, was the son of Violeta, one of my mother's half-sisters. He was not here to rent a room and watch over us, which was what our parents were in need of, but rather to hide from justice, having fled Guatemala under sinister circumstances.

My father's obsession with flashy new cars—a Camaro or a Mustang—and his fine suits for his yearly trips to Chicago, left our family still struggling to put food on the table. My mother, unable to quit her job, left us in the care of this man, whose presence would soon cast a shadow over my life.

Tito's arrival was anything but ordinary. He bore the scar of a bullet wound on his chest, a grim reminder of the life he had left behind. Though my mother refuses to speak of him or about this incident, I later learned the truth: Tito's father was one of Guatemala's most feared criminals, a ruthless gangster. Tito had undoubtedly brought money to ease our financial burden in Montreal, but at what cost? This was the man my parents trusted to watch over us while they were at work, a man running from his own demons, who would soon bring them into our home.

It pains me very much to revisit this episode. I was molested. Everyday of that horrible period in our lives I dreaded coming back home from school. I still feel my heart pound just picturing myself holding my brother's hand after picking him up after school and entering the hallway, taking the steps up to our apartment, knowing who is inside waiting for us and not knowing what will happen. Will he carry me on his lap and make me touch his bullet wound while he slips his hand into my panties or will he be entertained by making my brother tear pages out of his collection of Playboy magazines and lighting them on fire to toss into the toilet?

Like any innocent child enduring such a devastating experience, I internalized the blame, believing that somehow it was all my fault—that I was tainted, unworthy, and bad. Those dark memories, too painful to process, retreated to the farthest corners of my mind, buried deep within my subconscious. They remained hidden there, untouched and unresolved, for more than half a century. It wasn't until I embarked on the healing journey set in motion by *The Ultimate Teacher* that these memories resurfaced, demanding to be confronted and finally understood…and more importantly - forgiven.

The events of my early childhood, absorbed while my brain was still evolving and making sense of the world, left a profound and lasting imprint on my life. Watching my mother, who, despite being an adult, in my eyes behaved like a little girl, always subservient to the authority of others - particularly my dad's, which deeply affected me. Without realizing it, I internalized this dynamic, following in her footsteps for much of my adult life. I became the person who was subservient and intimidated by others, particularly by my husband. But fortunately midway through my life, in my fifties, I found the strength to assert myself, breaking free from those ingrained patterns, much like she did too.

My mother's endless, almost pathological devotion to taking care of my father—treating him as if he were a child— left a powerful impression. She sacrificed her children's needs in the process. In response, I took the opposite approach: my children would always come first. I vowed that no one, no situation, would ever cause me to abandon their well-being. My children would be my priority—always.

Reflecting on those early years, I realize how the awkwardness and fear I experienced during my First Confession, and the hollow ritual of my First Communion, marked the beginning of my growing awareness. Though I tried to be a good Catholic girl, I soon understood that Catholicism, and indeed no organized religion for that matter, would ever be my path. The rituals felt disconnected from reality, and I knew even then that I was searching for something deeper, something more authentic.

Witnessing the violence and civil unrest in Guatemala at such a tender age, especially the traumatic event at the Mayan School, also left a lasting impression. Comparing the stark contrast between the peaceful life in Montreal and the chaos of my homeland ignited a passion in me that would define much of my adult life: a deep commitment to justice and fairness. I became acutely aware of the inequalities faced by people based on economic or social class, race, ethnicity, and gender. This early sense of justice shaped my worldview and my desire to fight for the rights of the oppressed.

All these powerful experiences—shaped before I had even turned 10—signaled the end of my first phase as a woman. The phase of childlike wonder, where innocence reigned, came to a close all too soon. Studies in behavioral health now confirm what I've come to know personally—that the early years, even those before birth, have a profound impact on how we develop as individuals. There's no question that trauma can and does affect the developing brain.

Just as my mother had before me, I too became pregnant with my first child out of wedlock, bearing the weight of society's shame and the moral judgment that religion cast upon us. Like many women in my family before me, I felt "forced" into marriage as a young girl, not by anyone in particular but by the weight of expectations placed upon us.

But that's a story for a later chapter.

And so, the seeds of who I would become were sown in those early years, shaped by both the beauty and the pain of my childhood.

CHAPTER 6

*"All around you, people who've had their fathers,
mothers, brothers, sisters, or children 'disappeared'
into the muck of the counterinsurgency violence – the
secret nighttime detentions, the killing squads, the
tortured bodies found in gutters or on vacant lots.
These losses sat like ghostly stains on everyone's soul."*

– Francisco Goldman, "The Long Night of White Chickens"

The Montreal Children's Hospital became a place where my parents not only found professional success but also forged lasting friendships and built rewarding careers. My father, in particular, gained immense respect from his mentors and professors. His surgical skills were unmatched—he possessed a steady hand, sharp insight, and a wealth of knowledge, which together made him an extraordinarily talented surgeon.

One day, a special patient arrived on my father's surgical team. It was a complex case—a premature baby born with a severe heart condition that required immediate surgery. The procedure was delicate, not only because of the nature of the heart defect but also because of the baby's size. To put things into perspective, the open-heart chest wound would later be covered with a dressing no bigger than an ordinary band-aid, which spanned the tiny chest entirely. The team affectionately nicknamed the baby "Twiggy," after the famous 1960s model, known for her ultra-thin frame, marking a trend that shaped the world of fashion for decades to come. Miguel's hands, it seemed, were guided by angels that day, and the surgery turned out to be a complete success.

This triumph earned my father a lasting reputation, one that would follow him throughout the rest of his career. Miguel Ángel Martini Padilla became recognized as one of the most gifted surgeons, with accolades spanning across Montreal, the United States, and Guatemala. His growing reputation soon caught the attention of the University of Minnesota's medical school, particularly their pediatric cardiac unit, which was making strides in groundbreaking research. They invited him to join their team, and so, in the early 1970s, we moved from Montreal to Minneapolis, Minnesota.

At that time, I was 11 years old, just on the brink of entering adolescence. My body was beginning its transformation, and in many ways, so was my life. We made the journey by car, driving down from Canada to the U.S., with our most cherished belongings in tow—my father's car, his extensive wardrobe, and, of course, his ever-expanding library. I remember crossing the border, immediately sensing the difference between Canada and the United States. Even the English spoken by the border patrol officer struck me—it sounded foreign to my ears.

When my brother and I were enrolled in a public elementary school in Minneapolis, I distinctly recall the confusion that my accent caused. They assumed I was from Boston, of all places! Little did they know, we had just arrived from the bilingual city of Montreal, where our lives had been shaped by a world entirely different from the one we were about to enter.

This marked my first experience with co-ed education, and coming from an all-girls Catholic school in Montreal, it was quite a culture shock. Suddenly, I found myself sitting alongside boys, and it fascinated me to observe the interactions between them and us girls. It didn't take long for me to appreciate the dynamic, and I quickly embraced the idea of boys as equals, rather than as a separate, mysterious group. It was a refreshing change, and I enjoyed this newfound sense of balance in the classroom.

We had moved into an apartment complex near the Minneapolis airport, and as a result, many of our neighbors were pilots and stewardesses, as flight attendants were called at the time. I was absolutely captivated by them. Everything about their profession appealed to me—the idea of traveling all over the world, dressing sharply in their uniforms, and carrying themselves with such poise. I imagined myself in their shoes, jet-setting across the globe. When I mentioned my dream of becoming a stewardess to my father, his response mirrored the response my maternal grandfather had expressed towards my mother's aspirations years before. He dismissed the idea, saying, "Stewardesses are nothing but maids in the air." Still, this didn't deter me—not at first. So what if they were considered glorified maids? I loved the idea of the job. But then he mentioned having to clean up after passengers suffering from air sickness, specifically the part about cleaning up vomit—now *that* did put an abrupt end to my dream of flying the skies.

Life in Minnesota was vastly different from what we had known in Montreal. We had left behind a beautiful, culturally rich city and now found ourselves in the outskirts of Minneapolis, a place defined by nature more than history or art. Yet, in its own way, it offered a different kind of beauty. Our apartment complex was situated near a creek, a winding waterway that became the heart of our explorations. That creek became a playground for my brother, myself, and the other children who lived nearby during that first—and only—summer we spent in Minneapolis.

The creek was shallow enough for us to wade across, and

we soon developed a fondness for the creatures that inhabited its waters. Frogs, garden snakes, and daddy long-leg spiders were frequent companions in our adventures, and we roamed the area without fear. We became amateur naturalists, observing the behaviors of the animals around us. I remember watching the robins, noticing how they always seemed to favor the worms over the wild berries, unlike the other birds. Those afternoons by the creek were filled with discovery, and in many ways, they were magical. While Minnesota didn't have the cultural sophistication of Montreal, it offered something else—an immersion in the natural world, and for a child, that was just as captivating, if not more so.

In the center of the apartment complex, there was a swimming pool that quickly became one of our favorite places to hang out, especially during those long summer days. One late afternoon, we were enjoying the water when we noticed everyone else was getting out. The sky had turned cloudy, but it was still warm enough to swim, so my brother and I stayed in, relishing the peacefulness of the nearly empty pool. But as the wind began to pick up and grow stronger, my mom decided it was time to call it a day. We reluctantly climbed out and made our way back to our first-floor apartment.

That evening, Mom started preparing our favorite meal for when Dad was on call and wouldn't be home for dinner— TV dinners. The simple joy of these meals meant we could eat in front of the television, but when we turned on the TV, something unusual happened. Instead of a show, we saw a bright red warning message: TORNADO WARNING. Thinking it was just a glitch, we changed the channel, but every station displayed the same red letters. This was before the days of cable, and with only four or five channels to choose from, we quickly realized we wouldn't have any TV to go with our dinners. Disappointed, we turned the TV off, wondering what to do next.

As we sat at the table, a loud knock on the door startled us. Who could it be? When we opened the door, one of our concerned neighbors stood there, looking a bit frantic. She suddenly remembered that we were new to the area—foreigners, in fact—and likely didn't know the local drill. "Everyone's gathering in the basement," she informed us urgently. "There's a serious tornado warning." And just like that, we learned what a tornado was.

We quickly joined the others in the basement, huddled together as the storm raged outside. The air was thick with nervous energy, everyone anxiously waiting for the all-clear. When it was finally safe to come back up and venture outside, the scene that greeted us was nothing short of surreal. The parking lot looked like a battlefield—cars were tossed around like my brother's Matchbox toys, completely displaced from their spots. The Coca-Cola vending machine, a familiar fixture by the pool, was now submerged in the water, and massive trees had been ripped from the ground as though they were nothing more than flimsy toothpicks.

It was my first real encounter with the sheer power of nature, and from that moment on, I developed a deep fear of tornadoes. The destructive force we witnessed that day left an indelible mark on me, a reminder of how fragile everything could be in the face of nature's fury.

By the end of 1971, my father had risen to prominence as one of the leading cardiothoracic surgeons in the program at the University of Minnesota. His remarkable skills had caught the attention of a prestigious medical program in Houston, Texas, which was world-renowned for its advances in cardiothoracic surgery. They extended him an invitation to join their elite team, and this offer would have marked a significant milestone in his career.

As exciting as the opportunity was, it posed a logistical challenge—our car wasn't large enough to transport all of our belongings, particularly my father's ever-growing medical library, which had become a prized collection over the years. To solve this, Dad purchased a small truck, and we prepared for the long drive down to Houston. The four of us—my parents, my brother, and I—were packed tightly into the cabin, eager to explore our future home. We had plans to scout out neighborhoods and choose a house in Houston, with my brother and me both lobbying enthusiastically for one with a pool.

But before settling into our new life in Texas, my father had a different idea. He wanted to take us on a road trip to Guatemala to share the thrilling news with our extended family. This was meant to be a celebratory family vacation, a chance to reconnect with our roots before starting a new chapter in Houston.

However, what began as an exciting family trip quickly turned into a nightmare that none of us could have predicted. The joyous news of our move to Houston would never be shared as planned, and our lives took a drastic turn. The vacation spiraled into a series of unfortunate events, and we never made it back to Houston again.

After what felt like an interminable journey, we finally crossed the border into Guatemala, but not without enduring a long, tense overnight stay in the bustling Mexican border town of Tapachula. The delay at the border was nerve-wracking, stretching our patience to its breaking point as we waited for the border patrol to grant us entry. The hold-up seemed to stem from the unusual cargo we were carrying in our "family truck." Our vehicle, laden with household goods that encapsulated our life on the move. The sheer volume and nature of our load likely raised eyebrows among the border officials, prompting them to scrutinize every item meticulously.

It was 1971, and the tensions and corruption brought on by the civil war that had engulfed Guatemala for the past decade were palpable, particularly at critical points of intersection like the border. I vividly remember my impressionable eight-year-old brother mistaking the scene for Vietnam, his young mind taking in the sight of soldiers in their military uniforms, clutching their rusted rifles with an air of authority that was both intimidating and surreal.

At the border customs office, we faced yet another hurdle: the officers demanded paperwork we simply couldn't produce. In the end, our helplessness led us to relinquish most of our precious belongings as "mordida"—a bribe to the officers who were adept at sensing fear and vulnerability in travelers. All that remained were our clothes and my father's cherished books, a bittersweet victory in an already stressful situation.

Just when it seemed like all hope was lost, our grandparents came to the rescue. The sight of them waiting for us on the other side of the border filled me with an explosion of delight that I can still recall vividly. The relief was overwhelming, especially knowing I would no longer have to endure the cramped cabin of the truck. Instead, I could ride in the comfort of my grandparents' station wagon, a welcoming embrace amid the chaos we had just navigated.

The journey from Tapachula, Mexico, to Mazatenango, Guatemala, spanned roughly 80 miles southward, winding through the lush tropical flatlands of the Pacific coast. As we drove, the landscape shifted around us, revealing vibrant greenery and the promise of adventure ahead. Our destination was "Finca Dolores," my uncle's enchanting coffee and sugar cane farm, which stood out as one of my favorite places in the small world I knew at the time.

My uncle, Roberto, was married to Letty, my father's sister and my mother's classmate who had introduced them. This close family connection fostered a deep bond between our families. My cousin Bobby, just nine months my junior, and Elizabeth, who was around the same age as my brother, made every visit to Guatemala feel like a reunion filled with laughter and fun. The farm was our playground, brimming with opportunities for exploration and mischief.

I have countless fond memories of playing on the coffee "patios," expansive areas where freshly harvested coffee beans were laid out to sun-roast. The smooth cement of the patios, which were gently sloped, became our roller-skating haven, where we'd glide and laugh, lost in our youthful joy.

Adjacent to the patios was "La Toma," a man-made canal that coursed fresh water from a nearby river. It was here that the freshly picked coffee beans were dropped at the top of the incline, and with the force of the rushing water that carried them downward, it would strip away their skins in the process. This canal was another of our favorite spots, where we launched paper boats, navigating the powerful current with giddy excitement. However, the strength of the water commanded respect, and we were closely supervised to ensure our safety.

We were forbidden from entering the "trapiche," the heart of sugarcane production, where the stalks were crushed in a massive machine to extract their sweet juice. The air was filled with the heady aroma of sugar cane as it boiled down in a large vat, transforming into the sticky sweetness of sugar cane honey. I can still taste the warm honey served on the tip of a sugar cane stalk, a delightful treat that required us to blow on it for what felt like ages until it cooled enough to handle.

For my brother and me, the exposure to the natural wonders at Finca Dolores was pure bliss. Coming from the controlled environments of North America, we exploded with joy in the freedom and sensory experiences the farm provided. Each moment spent there felt like a precious gift, a reminder of the simple joys that nature can offer, and I cherished those days of adventure, discovery, and unfiltered happiness.

As the owner of the land, my uncle Roberto was known as a beloved and respected "terra-teniente." His laborers regarded him not only as their employer but also as a source of inspiration, feeling fortunate to work and live on his farm. The estate had been in his family for generations, a legacy he cherished deeply. Although he had a brother and a sister, neither showed any interest in taking over the farm, leaving the responsibility solely to him—a role he embraced with pride and enthusiasm.

Roberto was the embodiment of a dedicated farmer, rising before dawn and retiring early, mirroring the rhythms of the land and the seasons. Unlike many landowners in the area, who preferred to socialize at the club in downtown Mazatenango, he often chose to join his laborers in a friendly soccer match, fostering camaraderie and respect among them. He was a shy yet kind-hearted man, family-oriented and known for his good nature. He rarely indulged in heavy drinking or smoking, embodying the ideal of a humble farmer devoted to his work and his family.

However, the man we encountered upon our arrival at the farm after the tumultuous events at the border was a stark contrast to the Roberto we had known. We found him noticeably changed. Roberto was now drinking and smoking heavily, his demeanor anxious and distracted. A small transistor radio was permanently stationed by his side, tuned into a news station that seemed to dictate his every thought. His eyes flickered with worry as he listened intently, particularly focused on the results of the recent elections. When the name of the winner was announced—General Carlos Arana Osorio—Roberto's face fell, and the weight of fear was clear to see settle on his shoulders.

This shift in Roberto's character painted a stark picture of the changes unfolding in Guatemala. The once vibrant and joyful atmosphere of Finca Dolores felt overshadowed by an undercurrent of unease. The farm that had been a sanctuary of laughter and adventure now echoed with the uncertainty of a nation grappling with turmoil. It was a poignant reminder that even the most beloved places and the people within them can be profoundly affected by the tides of political change.

Arana Osorio marked the beginning of a troubling era in Guatemala as he became the first in a series of military dictators aligned with the PID (Partido Institucional Democrático) party. This party would go on to dominate Guatemalan politics for the next twelve years, largely through electoral fraud and manipulation. Unlike Jorge Ubico, who, despite his harsh rule, managed to establish some enduring institutions that still hold value in the country today, these new dictators were devoid of any redeeming qualities. They were deeply corrupt, having sold their souls to the highest bidder—primarily the frenzied and fearful anti-communist United States, as well as any other entity willing to fund their hold on power.

To fully understand this dark period, we must look back at a pivotal moment in history. In 1954, a coup orchestrated by the U.S. installed Carlos Castillo Armas, toppling the first democratically elected president, Juan Jose Arévalo, interestingly he was the father of the current president of Guatemala - Bernardo Arevalo. This event set off a chain reaction, ushering in a succession of right-wing military dictators who ruled through intimidation and deceit.

The consequences of this political upheaval were devastating, particularly regarding land distribution. Wealthy residents of European descent, those who had the resources to support these dictators, along with foreign companies like the American United Fruit Company, seized control of vast tracts of land. This unjust allocation of resources led to increasing tensions and conflicts with the rural poor, laying the groundwork for the Civil War that erupted in 1960. That year, a group of left-wing junior military officers attempted a revolt against General Ydigoras Fuentes, the fraudulent commander-in-chief at the time. Although this revolt failed, the surviving officers went on to form a rebel movement known as MR-13.

By the 1970s, Guatemala was embroiled in social unrest, primarily fueled by the government's oppressive tactics against various leftist rebel groups. Many of these insurgents were supported by ethnic Maya indigenous communities and Ladino peasants, particularly farm laborers. In their struggle for rights and recognition, they organized into guerilla factions, fighting back against the government's brutal repressions.

The conflict in Guatemala spiraled into a brutal period of oppression, where the government's grip tightened through violence and fear. During this dark chapter, an estimated 140,000 to 200,000 people were killed or forcibly "disappeared," with reports of up to 50,000 missing. My uncle Roberto was one of those who disappeared, a victim of a regime that crushed dissent with brutal efficiency. His disappearance became a stark reminder of the devastating cost of political oppression, a trauma that would leave an indelible mark on our family and the nation for generations.

The violence was not merely the result of a civil war between government forces and rebel groups but rather a calculated campaign of terror, orchestrated by military intelligence. Civilians—returning refugees, academics, students, leftist politicians, trade unionists, religious workers, and even street children—became targets in a systematic purge. Anyone perceived as a threat to the state, no matter how innocent, faced disappearance or death. In this climate of fear, my uncle, a compassionate farmer who simply cared for his workers, became an easy mark for the regime.

Roberto's disappearance, like countless others, was shrouded in terror. He was last seen with his trusted aide, Pablo, whose body was later found near their abandoned truck. All that remained of Roberto was a bloodied shirt on the driver's seat. Rumors of his fate began to circulate—some said he was thrown into the Motagua River, others believed he was dropped from a military helicopter into the crater of an active volcano, or into the Pacific Ocean. The truth, however, remained unknown, leaving a haunting void.

His absence devastated his family. Letty, his wife, was left to care for their five children, the youngest just a newborn of 40 days. With no support, she was evicted from both their farm and their home in Guatemala City, properties that had been seized and transferred to another family. This violent upheaval left my aunt destitute, her future and that of her children uncertain.

In the wake of this tragedy, my grandfather begged my father not to leave Guatemala. My father, torn between his prestigious position at a Houston hospital and the duty to support his shattered family, made the heart-wrenching decision to stay. This choice, driven by loyalty and love, forever altered the course of our lives, entwining us with the relentless grip of a nation gripped by terror.

CHAPTER 7

"You will always be Esperanza. You will always be Mango Street. You can't erase what you know. You can't forget who you are."

– Sandra Cisneros, "The House on Mango Street"

Shortly after settling in Guatemala, where my father had turned down a promising opportunity in Houston, another enticing offer emerged. During his annual international medical conferences at the McCormick Convention Center in Chicago, a visiting surgeon enticed my father with yet another prestigious opportunity: a chance to complete a cardiovascular surgical rotation at Johns Hopkins Hospital in Baltimore. This was an irresistible proposition that could greatly advance his career and professional reputation.

Even though my brother and I had already been enrolled in private schools; me at a Catholic all girls school - Instituto La Asuncion, and him at my father's old alma mater - Colegio La Preparatoria - an all boys school which had retained its reputation as one of the best academic institutions in the country since the 1940s, we still faced yet again a relocation of our lives and moved to Baltimore.

When we arrived in Baltimore my brother and I were enrolled in St. James Elementary, a co-ed private Catholic school. Due to the civil and racial unrest that Baltimore was going through at the time, public school was considered too risky so our lives became confined to the safe walls of our new suburban Catholic school and the walls of our small two-bedroom apartment on the eighth floor of a building located right on the edge of the racial divide in the city. The neighborhood was off-limits, leaving us with a childhood experience largely shaped by the routines of school and our compact living space.

After my father completed his rotation, we returned to Guatemala, where life briefly settled again. My father opened a private clinic and became one of the founding members of Hospital Centro Médico, a major private hospital in the country, and my brother and I returned to our previous schools. With extended family nearby and a lively neighborhood full of children our age, we finally found a sense of belonging and stability - at least for a brief moment in time.

Yet between 1970 and 1974, we were living in what I've come to call the "in-between zone." We were constantly navigating the complexities of two countries, two education systems, and two sets of cultural expectations. This period of being suspended between worlds deeply impacted us, shaping our identities and how we related to the world. Moving between cultures and environments left us in a state of flux, never fully grounded in one place or the other, always adapting and reshaping ourselves to fit.

Living in this duality brought both benefits and challenges, mirroring the complexity of life itself. The shifting between cultures gave me adaptability, a skill that would become invaluable as I entered young adulthood. During my teenage years, I began to stand out in our Guatemalan neighborhood, where my time in the United States had given me a more relaxed attitude toward friendships with boys, a rarity in the more conservative society around me. My peers affectionately called me "La Gringuita," viewing me as an American girl, a novelty that sparked curiosity.

"La Gringuita" - me at 13 years old

In Guatemala, I was comfortable speaking with boys as my peers in the neighborhood, something that was often met with jealousy from other girls. My fashion choices, like wearing miniskirts that were trendy in the U.S., further set me apart. This combination of openness and a more liberal attitude toward friendships made me both admired and scrutinized. While I enjoyed the attention, I also became the subject of harsh judgment from those who adhered more strictly to local cultural norms.

This experience of being caught between the cultural expectations of the U.S. and Guatemala highlighted the deep contrasts in how I was perceived. I often felt like an outsider in both places, misunderstood and judged in ways that exposed the complexities of identity. Navigating this cultural duality became a defining feature of my adolescence, shaping my understanding of who I was and how I fit into these two very different worlds. It forced me to reconcile seemingly opposing parts of myself.

In 1972, I embarked on a new academic journey at Colegio Evelyn Rogers, a progressive bilingual school that had recently opened its doors. The transition was significant, as 98% of my new classmates were familiar faces from La Asunción, the Catholic school I had previously attended. This mass migration from one institution to another was largely influenced by the socio-economic landscape of Guatemala's upper middle class at the time. Some of the girls hailed from families with deep-rooted wealth acquired through vast landholdings, while others, like myself, came from hardworking professional families striving to make their mark.

At Colegio Evelyn Rogers, I encountered two remarkable individuals who would become my lifelong friends: Maya and Anaite. Maya was the daughter of a highly intelligent and progressive lawyer, who later rose to become the Dean of Legal Studies at the esteemed University of San Carlos. Known for his impassioned advocacy for union trade workers, he tragically lost his life in 1977 when he was brutally murdered outside his office. That's how unstable and dangerous the political climate was at the time. Anaite, on the other hand, was the daughter of a soon-to-be-successful civil engineer, a proud descendant of Greek immigrants.

From the moment we met, Maya, Anaite, and I forged a bond so profound that it felt like we were sisters, destined to be in each other's lives forever. Neither of them had sisters, and I had just welcomed a little sister into the world, born in 1972 and 14 years my junior. Our friendship was a tapestry woven with shared experiences, laughter, and dreams, forming a strong foundation that would support us through the many challenges and triumphs that lay ahead.

I truly believed my father's relentless pursuit of board certifications and advanced surgical techniques had finally reached a satisfying conclusion. He had successfully established his private practice and became a founding associate of what would evolve into the prestigious Hospital Centro Medico in Guatemala. In a short time, he gained recognition as an exceptional surgeon and physician, returning to the country armed with cutting-edge surgical knowledge that had previously only been available to the wealthy Guatemalans who could afford to travel to the United States. Yet, despite his achievements, he continually grappled with the limitations of inadequate medical equipment.

In 1974, an opportunity arose when the Health Secretary, impressed by the surgery my father had performed on him, offered him a chance to acquire a fully equipped cardiac unit with the latest tools and gadgets. Eager to seize this rare opportunity, my father readily accepted the offer. However, there was a catch: it came with the stipulation that he would need to complete another year of residency in a hospital in Newark, New Jersey.

We relocated to Caldwell, New Jersey, with my father keeping us away from Newark, where his hospital was located, due to the city's struggles with drugs and racial tensions at the time. A well known story for us with our previous experience in Baltimore. This move, however, was met with a deep internal resistance from me. Unlike past transitions, this time I wished to be left behind. I didn't want to leave my school, my friends, my first boyfriend, or the comfort of our familiar upper-middle-class life in Guatemala City. The turbulence of racial tensions and civil unrest in New Jersey only deepened my sense of disconnection and frustration.

When I found myself enrolled in James Caldwell High School, a public school I quickly grew to loathe, my resistance hardened. I had left a beautiful private institution in Guatemala, only to enter an environment where police conducted surprise searches with K-9 units looking for drugs. The academic offerings were another bitter disappointment. Back home, I had been taking advanced courses in philosophy and biopsychology, and here, nothing challenged or inspired me. It felt like my world was shrinking.

This chapter of our lives didn't feel like progress; it felt like unraveling. My father's professional achievements offered little solace as I navigated an unsettling new environment. Alienation seeped into my days, amplifying a growing sense of dislocation. In an act of rebellion, I made the bold decision to drop out of school. Instead of the punishment I had expected, my parents surprised me by ordering textbooks from my school in Guatemala so I could homeschool myself. This unconventional arrangement offered a sense of relief, a chance to reclaim some control.

My days settled into a routine of helping my mother with chores, caring for my two-year-old sister, and immersing myself in studies intended for my return to Guatemala. I wrote weekly letters to my friends back home and lost myself in oil paint-by-number sets in my free time. Yet, beneath this surface routine, I felt the first stirrings of depression. It wasn't just discomfort from being "in-between" cultures anymore; it was a profound sense of disconnection. I had lost the ties that once grounded me—my belonging, and my sense of connection.

Then, one evening, the doorbell to our apartment unit rang while we were having dinner. I answered the intercom, and to my amazement, it was my grandfather's voice! He and my grandmother had decided to surprise us by stopping in New Jersey on their way back to Guatemala after a trip they had just completed in Europe. Their surprise visit felt like a lifeline, a bridge back to the world I so desperately missed. I confided in my grandmother, who had always been my closest ally, sharing my deep desire to leave New Jersey. She listened with the same nurturing wisdom I had relied on since childhood, and within days, something shifted.

Plans were soon underway for my brother and me to return to Guatemala with our grandparents when they left. The news filled me with overwhelming joy. I was leaving behind the disconnection and heading back to the life I adored—my school, my friends, and the familiar embrace of my homeland. Back in Guatemala, surrounded by my peers, I felt whole again. The warmth and familiarity of my roots wrapped around me, dispelling the discontent that had weighed me down in New Jersey. I had returned home, to the place where I felt I truly belonged.

Once I was back in Guatemala, on a bright Saturday afternoon, my attention was drawn to a striking young man on a motorcycle—a face completely unfamiliar in our tight-knit neighborhood where everyone knew each other. Intrigued by his mysterious presence, I asked around and learned his name was Carlos. He had just returned from studying in the United States, making him feel to me like a kindred spirit, someone who might understand the complexities of my own life.

Curiosity led me into his orbit, and soon, I found myself in his company. Carlos, with his long hair and captivating smile, seemed taken by me, too. His white Fiat became a familiar sight, often waiting for me at my bus stop, a signal of his growing interest. One day, as we stood close, he leaned in and kissed me. The jolt of that kiss was electric, like a lightning bolt through my veins. My heart raced, my cheeks burned, and my knees felt weak. In that instant, Carlos had captured more than just my heart—he had taken hold of my soul.

Before long, Carlos became the center of my world. He was the first thought I had every morning and the last one before I fell asleep. Everything else—school, friends, parties, even family—faded into the background, eclipsed by the intensity of my feelings for him. Just hearing his voice sent a surge of excitement through me, filling a void I hadn't even realized was there. I felt like the luckiest person in the world, intoxicated by the idea that we were breathing the same air.

CHAPTER 8

"When we love, we always strive to become better than we are. When we strive to become better than we are, everything around us becomes better too."

– Paulo Coelho, The Alchemist

1976

1976 stands out as one of the most pivotal years of my life. It began with an earth-shattering event—literally. At 3:01 a.m. on February 4th, a massive 7.5-magnitude earthquake ripped through Guatemala, its epicenter along the Motagua Fault, about 160 kilometers northeast of Guatemala City in Izabal. Though it only lasted for about 30 to 40 seconds, the devastation it caused was unimaginable. In that brief span, 23,000 lives were lost, and thousands more were left homeless. It was, without question, the most catastrophic disaster to strike Guatemala in modern times. It's difficult to convey how much can happen in less than a minute, but the aftermath of that earthquake reshaped the lives of countless people.

The night before the quake, on February 3rd, we had been sitting at the dinner table, engrossed in a conversation about the ongoing territorial dispute between Great Britain and Guatemala over Belize. This conflict dated back to a treaty from 1859, which both countries had interpreted differently over the years. By 1976, tensions were escalating, with threats being exchanged between government officials. My father, casually discussing the matter over dinner, remarked, "What is Guatemala thinking? If war broke out, Great Britain could send just a couple of fighter jets and wipe out our entire military."

For my 13-year-old brother, this offhand comment planted vivid, terrifying images of fighter jets attacking Guatemala. He went to bed that night haunted by these thoughts. I, at 17, thought he was being childish. My mind, however, had its own demons to grapple with. Ever since I had watched *The Exorcist* I had been deeply traumatized, convinced that some dark force might one day possess me.

We had recently moved to a two-story house on Avenida Las Américas, close to the airport, having left our old neighborhood as my father's career and social status elevated our family beyond the middle class. It was a bittersweet move for me because it meant leaving behind Carlos, the long-haired, motorcycle-riding boy who had stolen my heart. To my parents, he was a rebellious hippie, but to me, he was everything.

That night, my three-year-old sister Ginna was restless and, after having a bad dream, crawled into bed with my parents. In doing so, she locked the door to the room we shared, leaving me alone. At 3:01 a.m., the first sounds of the earthquake reached us—a low rumbling that, at first, my father mistook for a speeding car. He was waiting for the inevitable crash when the tremors hit.

Suddenly, the power went out, plunging the entire city into darkness. The house began to shake violently, not just side to side but also up and down, as if the earth itself had turned into a wild, furious beast trying to throw us all off. My father, who had been awake and studying, leaped into action. My mother clutched my little sister tightly in her arms, disoriented, and tried to seek refuge in her closet. My father quickly redirected them toward the door, shouting for my brother and me to get out of our rooms. "A volcano is being born!" he yelled, his voice filled with urgency.

In our rooms that night, my brother and I were trapped in the grip of our own imagined horrors. Terrified by the dinner conversation, he cowered under his bed, screaming, "The English are attacking us!" Meanwhile, I lay paralyzed, the tremors coursing through my bed convincing me I was possessed by the devil—just like the girl in *The Exorcist*.

The power of suggestion, fueled by the groundbreaking special effects of the film and the weight of ingrained guilt, utterly consumed me. Back then, I saw God as vengeful and punishing, and I was convinced I had crossed some unspoken line. The Catholic Church's condemnation of *The Exorcist* only added to the allure for my friends and me. Long before the film's release, we had devoured the book, making the eventual experience of watching it all the more harrowing.

When the bed began to shake violently in the pitch-black stillness of my room, accompanied by an eerie rumbling unlike anything I'd ever known, it wasn't just fear that gripped me—it was certainty. The images and beliefs deeply etched in my young mind left no room for doubt. I *was* possessed. And that conviction, born of cultural taboos and vivid storytelling, lingered long into adulthood, shaping my reality in ways I didn't yet understand.

It was a surreal and terrifying moment, one in which our deepest fears—fueled by our imaginations—merged with the very real horror of the earthquake.

With a sudden jolt, we were pulled back into the terrifying reality unfolding around us. But what exactly was happening? The world outside was a black, dusty void, and the second story of our house swayed like a ship caught in a violent storm. Every step we took felt precarious as we struggled to stay on our feet and find our way to the staircase. Our only thought was to get out of the house before it collapsed on top of us.

It's hard to put into words the emotions that surge through you when faced with something of such overwhelming force. Your instincts scream at you to run for safety, yet your mind frantically tries to grasp what's happening, searching for any rational explanation. Panic and confusion wage a war within you, but survival kicks in.

Mom took charge, leading us down the stairs while counting each step. Dad stayed at the back, shielding us from falling debris, which he thought were ceiling lamps crashing down. The house creaked and groaned as we made our way down, the fear of it collapsing growing with every second. When we finally reached the first floor, Mom handed me the statues of the Holy Family—Jesus, Mary, and Joseph—that had sat on the entrance table. We had just finished praying the novena two days earlier, on February 2nd, as was our family tradition. She tasked me with protecting them and starting a prayer. But in my state of shock, I could barely form the words. All I could manage was, "Our Father who art in Heaven..." before my mind went blank. The rest of the prayer dissolved in my mind.

Once outside, Dad directed us to our family cars, and he quickly moved them onto the meridian in the middle of the wide avenue. It was the safest place—away from any structures that could fall and crush us. The tension was thick, and even though we were out of the house, fear still gripped us. We weren't sure if more tremors were coming or if we were truly safe yet.

Our two beloved maids, Juanita and Chusita, emerged from their quarters. Chusita cradled our new German Shepherd puppy, Smoky, tightly in her arms, while Juanita carried our two Dachshunds, Snoopy and Susy. They had come through the kitchen, where all the cabinets had swung open and their contents had crashed to the floor, creating a dangerous mess of shattered glass. Yet somehow, miraculously, both women had walked barefoot across the debris without a single scratch, as if they had glided over it.

Once Dad made sure we were safe outside, he knew his work wasn't done. The trauma hospital would need him desperately, and there was no time to waste. He took one of our cars, and left to face the overwhelming tragedy unfolding across the country. For the next two days, we didn't see him. When he finally returned, it was only for a brief respite—just a few hours of rest before he went back to confront the horrors that continued to emerge after the earthquake.

The tremors, or aftershocks, were relentless. They rattled the city for the rest of the month, some gentle and fleeting, others sharp and violent enough to bring down buildings already weakened by the initial quake. It was too dangerous to go back inside, let alone return to school. Inspections of public buildings, including schools, were slow and painstaking, as every structure had to be evaluated for damage. So we stayed outdoors, improvising a new way of living.

My brother and I made a valiant attempt to pitch a tent on our front lawn, but it was a disaster—flimsy and inadequate against the elements. That's when Carlos, my knight in shining armor, came to the rescue. With skill and precision, he set up a sturdy tent using lazos and blankets. He transformed our chaotic yard into a cozy refuge, even setting up my portable record player so I could feel like a genie tucked away in a magical lamp, surrounded by pillows and nestled on top of soft rugs. It was enchanting—and incredibly romantic in the eyes of my 17-year-old self.

Carlos didn't stop there. He brought us coal for the grill, as power outages had become the norm, and he ensured we had enough food and water to get by. In the absence of my father, who was tirelessly caring for others at the hospital, Carlos became our protector and provider. I was completely and utterly smitten with him. He was my hero.

Meanwhile, Colegio Evelyn Rogers, perched on a high mountain on the road to El Salvador at kilometer 8, remained closed. The buildings, though newly constructed, needed to be inspected for structural damage, and the backlog of inspections meant a long wait. In response, our school devised a workaround: we were to visit once a week to collect materials for our courses. We would complete the assignments at home and return the following week to submit them and pick up new work.

What seemed like a reasonable plan quickly became overwhelming. Each of our teachers assigned more work than we could manage, and with 12 courses to cover in a bilingual program, the workload was immense. On top of that, as seniors, we had additional responsibilities: a class seminar on a social issue and a private thesis in either math and science or literature and social sciences. The diploma we were working towards, the *Bachiller en Ciencias y Letras*, was no ordinary high school diploma. It was equivalent to a bachelor's degree, allowing graduates to go straight into university-level studies in fields like medicine, law, architecture, and engineering, without needing to attend college first.

To make matters worse, not all of the textbooks we needed had arrived in Guatemala before the earthquake, and their delivery was now delayed indefinitely. I struggled to keep up, partly due to the lack of resources but mostly because my heart and mind were no longer focused on school. My thoughts were consumed by Carlos.

It was no secret that many young couples found themselves expecting children in the aftermath of the earthquake. Perhaps the proximity to death made people cling more fiercely to life, or perhaps the trauma left everyone seeking comfort in the arms of others. Whatever the reason, Carlos and I became part of that statistic. In the local slang, we had "metido las patas"—we had stumbled and fallen headfirst into a situation we weren't ready for.

At 17, I was pregnant in my senior year of high school. Carlos, at 19, was just beginning his first year of architecture school. We were still children ourselves, pretending to be adults in a relationship we barely understood. We didn't know how to take care of ourselves, let alone the child we were now bringing into the world. I was terrified—mostly of my father. I was convinced that once he found out, he would either disown me or, worse, kill Carlos. I truly believed he was capable of such extremes.

In an attempt to stay in denial, I confided only in my closest friends, Anaite and Maya. They both agreed that I needed to confirm if I was really pregnant, but in those days, home pregnancy tests weren't available. The only way to find out was through a lab test, and I couldn't risk going to one of the city's hospital labs where my father would undoubtedly hear about it.

Somehow, my friends managed to find a discreet private owned lab, and together we hatched a plan. Maya even lent me her grandmother's wedding band so I would look more "respectable" when we went, a laughable matter in hindsight when I remember how we must have really looked with our school bags and youthful appearance. We were in the middle of our midterm exams which meant as soon as we finished the examination of the day we could leave the school. One of our friends owned a car so as soon as we finished our test for that day we made a detour to the lab. I brought my urine sample in a baby food jar that Chusita had sterilized for me, and we carried on with our plan, hoping for the best, but bracing for whatever the results would bring.

When the results were handed to me, I rushed back to my friend's car where Maya and Anaite were anxiously waiting for me to open the envelope. My hands trembled as I tore it open, and there it was, staring back at me in black and white: "Positive." The silence that followed was deafening. "Now what?" I muttered, as the weight of those words sank in. Without hesitation, we headed straight for the nearest bar, "Baby's Beer"—an ironic twist given my newfound predicament.

Inside the dimly lit bar, my legs shook uncontrollably as I sat in front of a mug of beer I had no intention of drinking. My mind raced. What should I do next? How would I tell Carlos? And my parents—how could I ever face them? With my thoughts spiraling, I asked to be dropped off at my grandparents' house. I wasn't ready to confront my own home, not yet.

My grandmother, wise and compassionate, took one look at me as I stepped through the door and instantly knew. "You're pregnant, aren't you?" she said softly, her eyes filled with understanding. How could she possibly know?! But she did. As I collapsed into her arms, the tears I had been holding back began to flow. She hugged me tightly and whispered reassurances that everything would be alright. To my astonishment, she confided that my parents had "metido las patas" too back in their day. I was stunned. I had never realized that their wedding in February 1958 had taken place just five months before I was born. It was a revelation that grounded me for a moment, but there was still the matter of my predicament.

At the time, Carlos had already dropped out of architecture school after just one semester and had taken a well paid job as a bilingual receptionist at a Canadian construction company that was building a nickel mine in the Atlantic coast of Guatemala called Exmibal. When I called him that evening from my grandparents' house, he agreed to meet me there since he lived in the same neighborhood they did. I braced myself for the conversation, hoping for some reassurance. When Grandpa returned from work, Grandma wasted no time in filling him in on my situation. Then, Carlos arrived. I got into his car, handed him the envelope with the lab results, and waited for his response. He didn't say a word, but his silence was deafening. All he said was, "Get out of the car please" as he left leaving me behind in a stunned state.

Those weeks that followed were some of the darkest of my very young life. Fear, anxiety, uncertainty, doubt, and sadness became my constant companions. I was terrified of my father's reaction—certain he would disown me or worse—and paralyzed by anxiety about school, my friends, and the judgment I knew was waiting for me from the community. The uncertainty of my future loomed large, and doubt consumed me: could I really go through with this? Despair overwhelmed me as I realized I had nowhere to turn. But perhaps the most crushing realization was that my feelings for Carlos were not mutual. The love I had for him was not returned in the same way, and that truth was devastating.

It would take me years—decades even—to fully understand and forgive both Carlos and myself for what our futures held. We were just children, scared out of our minds, each of us reacting in our own way. Carlos' response was to run, something that would become a pattern for him throughout his life. Meanwhile, I, despite my efforts to accommodate his wishes, found that my motherly instincts were far stronger than the love I had for him.

On the day I was supposed to meet an illegal abortionist, I found a strength I didn't know I had. I told Carlos he was free to go, that I didn't need him. "The Martini surname will be enough for my baby," I said. It was a bold statement, one that would prove to be prophetic in the years to come.

With Carlos gone, the time came to face my father. I had dreaded this moment more than anything, and when it came, it was as awful as I had feared. He reacted with anger and disappointment, but instead of the disownment I had anticipated, he simply said, "I am completely disappointed in you." Those words cut deeper than any punishment. They would haunt me for much of my life, fueling a deep sense of shame and failure that I would carry for years.

Facing my school's owner and director, Evelyn Rogers, was another hurdle. I wanted nothing more than to drop out and finish my senior year after the baby was born, but Evelyn had other plans. Masking her disdain with feigned concern for my education, she sweet-talked my parents into letting me stay in school. She made it clear that she wouldn't stand by and watch me throw away my future, so she "graciously" allowed me to continue attending school, despite my pregnancy.

While I grappled with the chaos in my life, Carlos was busy devising his own plan. He decided to leave the country and go to Los Angeles to live with his uncle. Little did I know that while he was making his arrangements, my aunt Thelma took it upon herself to visit Carlos' house and spill the beans to his parents, who were completely unaware of the situation. Carlos' father, appalled and humiliated by his son's actions, insisted that Carlos ask for my hand in marriage. According to him, it was the only way to restore my honor.

But my father wasn't having it. He flat-out refused to marry me off to a man who had already shown such little regard for me. However, after many drinks and long conversations with his lawyer, his best friend, and my grandparents, he relented. In the end, it was decided that we would marry. Why endure the shame and finger-pointing any longer? To the outside world, we were the "lovebirds" who had simply made a mistake. And so, our fates were sealed.

Carlos' father bought the ring, and my mother sprang into action. Within a month, she orchestrated a grand wedding for 150 guests. It was as if she were on autopilot, determined to make it a perfect event despite the circumstances. On June

26, 1976, Carlos and I were married at St. Jude's Church. The ceremony was followed by a lavish reception at Club Americano, complete with two live bands. Invitations were printed and hand-delivered to everyone of importance, including the sitting vice president of the country. The event was a spectacle, Carlos and I were like marionettes, going through the motions without any real emotional connection to what was happening. We were told where to sit, what to say, when to smile, when to eat, and when to dance. My mother even gave us money for a honeymoon.

"Carlos and me – wedding picture, June 26, 1976"

When the honeymoon ended, reality set in. It was a cold shock—two young people now thrust into adult life, but standing on opposite ends of the spectrum. Carlos clung to his boyhood, while I was faced with the enormous responsibility of bringing a new life into the world. As Carlos regressed, puffing out his chest to mask his insecurities, he marked his territory like a child trying to prove something, while we were left to deal with the consequences of our situation.

The first day I returned to school, the tone was set immediately. It became clear why I had been allowed back despite being both married and pregnant, which was - the prized tuition fees - that this new school still under development desperately needed. At home, my father's disappointment weighed on me like a heavy shadow, his words—"I am completely disappointed in you"—still echoing in my ears. He had made it clear that in his house, his rules were law. And that didn't sit well with Carlos, who believed he should be the one in control of me. The tension between them grew, each man vying for dominance, using me as the pawn in their silent war.

Living with my parents was inevitable—Carlos and I had almost no income. It was decided, though unspoken, that I would remain in my parents' house, stuck between two men battling for authority over me. My father believed I was under his command, while Carlos, my new husband, demanded the same respect. It escalated to absurd levels, and I was the casualty, torn between their egos. Everywhere I turned, I saw only reflections of a lost, frail, scared girl—a child-woman who couldn't please anyone. Carlos resented the life he never wanted, and my father's disappointment radiated in everything he did. There was no escape.

Even at school, I faced another tormentor—Evelyn Rogers, the school director and owner. She had made up her mind to make my life as difficult as possible. In her view, I was an embarrassment, and she was determined to punish me for it. She even sent me to the school psychologist, convinced that I must be crazy to have allowed myself to get pregnant. Carlos was banned from stepping foot on school grounds. In spite of all this, I tried to focus on my studies. I had always enjoyed learning, even if I wasn't an honor student, and I poured my energy into my classes.

Our senior seminar was on the socio-economic problems the country was facing in the aftermath of the earthquake—a timely and important subject. Resources for our project were plentiful, coming directly from current events, not from books or libraries. The nightly news was our primary source, and I threw myself into the assignment, determined to do my part. By the time we were set to present our work to the public, I was seven months pregnant. My body had long outgrown my teenage clothes, and for the first time, I wore a proper maternity dress.

Standing beside my classmates, I was proud of the work we had done. We had worked hard, and I had contributed just as much as anyone else. But it didn't matter. The audience's focus wasn't on the presentation—it was on me, or more specifically, my pregnant belly. The whispers were loud enough to hear. Parents could barely concentrate on the project because all eyes were on me. I had unintentionally become the center of attention, and it wasn't for my academic contribution.

Evelyn Rogers was furious. She threw a tantrum, her frustration palpable as the attention shifted from the seminar to the spectacle of my pregnancy. In her eyes, I had stolen the spotlight, and it was unforgivable. But in that moment, standing there with my classmates, I felt the weight of what my life had become. No matter how hard I tried to fit in or contribute, I would always be the girl who got pregnant, the girl who disappointed everyone.

Soon after our seminar presentation, the final examinations loomed ahead. Evelyn Rogers was determined not to allow me to graduate with my class, knowing that my presence would draw attention to what she viewed as a scandalous situation. She had made it her personal mission to ensure that I would not stand on that stage alongside my classmates. To her, I was a disgrace, and she couldn't stomach the idea of me shifting the focus of graduation night from academic achievement to what she deemed an embarrassing example of improper behavior. Some of the parents from high society shared her concern, worried that my appearance might cast a shadow over the school's reputation and set a "bad example" for their daughters. The whispering and societal shame became a storm they sought to avoid.

So, a plan was quietly hatched between Evelyn Rogers and one of the professors—Vicente Chapero, the philosophy teacher. He, unlike the others, was willing to go along with Rogers' scheme. Vicente would later rise to become the director of the school, but at that time, he was simply a pawn in her strategy. Philosophy had turned out to be one of the most difficult subjects for me, largely because I never had the textbook. At home, the ongoing battle between my father and Carlos often turned into a tug-of-war over financial responsibilities. The textbook became another item they argued over—who should pay for it—and in the end, I never got the book at all. Although I worked hard in class, took detailed notes, and participated as best I could, when it came time for grading, I fell short—by a single point.

That one point meant I wouldn't pass the course, and because of that, I wasn't allowed to graduate with my class of 1976. Evelyn Rogers had succeeded in her mission. She never lost the tuition fees my attendance provided while she "set me as an example" of bad behavior and its consequences. The only glimmer of hope offered to me was the opportunity to retake the examination, but it wouldn't be until the next school term, in January of 1977. By then, my life had changed dramatically. On December 17, 1976, I gave birth to my beautiful baby boy, and my world turned upside down in ways I couldn't have imagined.

Two weeks after giving birth, I found myself back in the

hospital, this time suffering from a serious case of mastitis in one of my breasts. The infection was painful and debilitating, and the demands of motherhood made it nearly impossible for me to even think about retaking that exam. My baby needed me, my body was weak, and the opportunity to reclaim my education slipped through my fingers. There was no more talk of the exam, no more chances to make up for that single point that had barred me from graduating.

The year 1976 had become a watershed moment —a year that would define me for decades to come. It began with the earthquake, a natural disaster that had shaken the entire country, and ended with a personal earthquake of my own: marriage, a failed attempt at graduating, and becoming a mother. Each event, in its own way, marked me, carving deep lines into my heart and soul. What could have been a year of celebration and accomplishment became a year of loss, struggle, and transformation. It was a year that would haunt me, but also shape the person I was becoming—a young mother, facing life without the safety net I once thought I had.

On December 17, 1976, at precisely 6:20 p.m., a beautiful and healthy baby boy was born into the world. Nothing could have prepared me for the waves of labor pain. I was convinced that I wouldn't survive the ordeal. But instead of dying, something miraculous was happening—I was being reborn, right alongside my son. While he was taking his first breath in this world, I was stepping into the new and all-encompassing role of "mother," a role that would shape my identity and be my constant source of joy and refuge for many years to come.

"Our first born, Carlos (Canche) born on December 17, 1976"

The joy surrounding my son's birth was palpable. As the first grandson and great-grandson in the Martini family, he quickly became the center of attention, just as I had been when I was born. He held a special place in the hearts of everyone, though perhaps my father was affected by becoming a grandfather in his early 40s. He wasn't ready to embrace the role—it made him feel old, a title he wasn't prepared for. In an effort to defy time and reclaim his youth, he and my mother made the surprising decision to have another child.

Amidst all of this, my son's birth marked the beginning of a new chapter in my life—one that redefined my priorities, my relationships, and my sense of self. As a mother, I felt both vulnerable and powerful. The innocence of my youth was slipping away, replaced by a fierce, unbreakable love for this new life I had brought into the world.

PART 2

CHAPTER 9

"(In my sleep I dreamed this poem)
Someone I loved once gave me a box full of darkness.
It took me years to understand that this, too, was a gift."

- Mary Oliver

My mother and I found ourselves in an unusual situation—pregnant at the same time, navigating our way through obstetrician appointments together and later visiting the same pediatrician. By the time my mother gave birth to my youngest sister, Myriam, the two newborns, were born just five months apart. One might think this overlap would bring us closer as a family, but the reality was quite different.

Rather than bonding over the shared experience of motherhood, a deep undercurrent of tension permeated our household. My mother and I were left to care for the babies, while my father and my husband became engulfed in their own personal rivalry. The tension between them wasn't born from the typical challenges of family life—it was driven by ego, pride, and a competition of masculinity. My father's growing success as a surgeon, which brought him increasing recognition and an elevated social status, only exacerbated the problem. As he attended more social events, where alcohol flowed freely, the pressure in our household built up like a tightly wound spring. Alcohol soon became a regular fixture, seeping into every corner of our lives, bringing with it a corrosive, degrading energy. What should have been a time of joy, nurturing new life, was overshadowed by resentment and emotional distance.

For the next 32 years, Carlos and I remained married, despite the underlying strain that marked much of our relationship. We brought two more children into the world— our daughter, Myriam Stella (whom we affectionately call "Beba"), born in 1982, and our son, Daniel, born in 1989. With each child, I felt the overwhelming desire to fulfill my role as a mother deepen. In those years, motherhood became not just a responsibility but the core of my identity. I craved affirmation, a validation that I was fulfilling the fundamental purpose of my life as a woman.

"Our daughter, Myriam Stella (Beba) born on October 4, 1982"

"Our youngest son, Daniel (Danny) born on November 25, 1989"

This yearning was not merely about receiving approval from a partner; it reflected a powerful instinctual need tied to my femininity. I had entered the fourth phase of womanhood, where the drive to procreate, nurture, and care for others consumed much of my emotional energy. This stage of my life wasn't just about wanting a romantic connection—it was about embracing the full essence of what it meant to be a woman. My identity became inseparable from my ability to give life, to care for my children, and to feel needed and valued by the people I loved. Being a mother gave me a profound sense of purpose and fulfillment, something that defined me deeply. It was a time of emotional awakening, where the drive to nurture life became the central axis around which my world revolved.

Despite the love I poured into my children and my desire to create a stable home, the external pressures of society began to take their toll. We spent much of our time at my parents' house, not only because our children were close in age but also because being with them allowed us access to the comforts and luxuries we couldn't afford on our own. My father's social circle was filled with the wealthiest of the wealthy, and attending these high-society gatherings became a regular part of our lives. However, what seemed like glamorous events were, in reality, breeding grounds for excess and indulgence.

At these parties, the air was thick with cigarette smoke, and alcohol was always within arm's reach. These temptations weren't just casual indulgences—they became crutches, not only for my father and Carlos but for my mother and me as well. Over time, the destructive habits that characterized these gatherings began to infiltrate our lives, eroding the foundation of what should have been a family focused on love and growth. The people around us, fueled by addiction and hedonism, became mirrors of our own struggles, and we found ourselves caught in a cycle of dependency that none of us could break free from.

The 1980s were a decade steeped in indulgence and excess, where boundaries blurred and the lines between right and wrong often dissolved into a haze. Our lives mirrored the times—unstructured, unhealthy. Beneath the surface of our seemingly ordinary existence, we were wrestling with silent battles, each of us carrying scars and trauma that we dared not share, even with one another.

The only genuine source of happiness in my life came from my children. Pouring all my attention into them became my refuge, and in return, they showered me with unconditional love. That love was my lifeline, the one thing that brought me joy amidst the chaos and instability surrounding us. While everything else felt like it was teetering on the edge of collapse, the bond I shared with my children was the one thing that felt real and unshakable.

In the midst of all this, I felt an overwhelming sense of powerlessness. I had no real autonomy, no control over my own life. Every decision I made seemed to be dictated by someone else—whether it was the expectations of my husband, the needs of my children, or the societal pressures that loomed over me. I was living someone else's life, fulfilling a role that had been thrust upon me, not one I had chosen for myself. This lack of control left me feeling suffocated, trapped in a world where I couldn't even hear my own voice. I was like a passenger on a train, watching life pass me by without ever being able to take hold of the reins.

The frustration of living a life that didn't align with my true desires began to gnaw at me, creating a deep sense of disconnection. I started to fantasize about breaking free—about leaving Carlos and stepping into a new life where I could finally live for myself. I pictured a future where, once the children were grown, I could carve out a space that belonged to me alone. But as much as I longed for that freedom, I knew deep down I wasn't ready. I had spent so many years defining myself as a mother that I couldn't yet see who I was outside of that role. The idea of leaving seemed like a distant dream, one I wasn't equipped to make a reality. And the only other option—returning to my parents' house—was unthinkable.

I wanted independence, but it felt so far out of reach. Before I could even begin to imagine a life on my own terms, I knew I needed to find the strength and resources to stand on my own. And at that point, I didn't have either.

Then, slowly but surely, things took a darker turn. Strange and menacing phone calls started coming to the house, filled with threats that sent chills down my spine. At the same time, Carlos began disappearing without explanation. Days would pass without any word from him, and when he finally returned, he offered no insight into where he had been or what he had been doing. The silence was deafening, and it only added to the growing sense of unease.

Our financial situation became increasingly unstable. We could never seem to pay the rent on time, which led us to move from place to place, never truly settling. Carlos, ever the charmer, made promises of better days ahead—of a steady income, stability, and a future where everything would fall into place. But these promises were nothing more than empty words. He never provided any clear answers about what was really happening.

As the years went on, it became painfully clear that our lives were built on nothing but fragile hopes, always on the verge of shattering. The weight of secrets, lies, and unfulfilled promises was becoming too much to bear. And through it all, I was left clinging to the remnants of a life I wasn't sure I even wanted, uncertain of how to move forward or where I truly belonged.

In 1989, as our lives were teetering on the edge—both emotionally and financially—I discovered I was pregnant with our youngest child. An event that brought me so much joy but at the same time fear. How could I possibly support another child when we were already struggling just to survive? I couldn't rely on Carlos. When it came to raising our children, I had long accepted that the burden fell solely on me. The weight of providing, nurturing, and ensuring their future was mine to carry alone.

For several years, I had been working as an English teacher at my children's school—not because I was a trained educator, but out of sheer necessity. My "professional" background was actually in translation, the only work I could do because of my lack of formal education but with a high understanding of the English language. I worked for a non profit religious organization named Christian Children's Fund, translating letters to and from the indigenous children in remote areas of the country and their mostly American sponsors. They paid me $0.25 per letter and every week I would translate between 100 - 200 letters on average. But when Carlos failed to provide the money for tuition, our children's education was suddenly at risk. The thought of them being pulled out of school terrified me, so once again, my English skills became my lifeline.

I found myself standing in front of a classroom, teaching 5th and 6th graders in exchange for tuition fees as compensation. It wasn't what I had imagined doing with my life, but at that point, it didn't matter. My role as a mother meant everything to me, and I would have done anything to ensure my kids got the education they deserved. Though teaching wasn't my original calling, I poured myself into the work and discovered I had a natural talent for teaching.

However, with this unexpected pregnancy, our already fragile financial situation crumbled further. It felt like we were drowning. The utilities were constantly being shut off, and there were weeks when I wasn't sure how to put food on the table. I kept working at the school my children attended, thankful they at least had access to an education, but everything else was unraveling. To make ends meet I took on extra tutoring jobs after school. Every penny was carefully dedicated for the baby—diapers, bottles, formula, clothes— to prepare for the arrival of our third child.

Obviously, the stress was overbearing and it actually affected my poor innocent unborn child when one day I ended up with a severe cardiac arrhythmia which landed me in the ER just a month away prior to giving birth. Thankfully, the doctors were able to control the situation, although I always felt like I had somehow failed to provide a peaceful environment in which my baby could develop comfortably.

Danny made his entrance into the world on November 25, 1989, just a day after we had watched the *Batman* movie starring Michael Keaton and Jack Nicholson. I've always joked that his love for the Dark Knight must have been so powerful that, even in the womb, he couldn't resist coming out to see it. In some strange way, I felt like his soul connected with the dark, lonely world of Bruce Wayne—the orphan turned hero, misunderstood but dedicated to fighting for justice. Although Danny wasn't literally an orphan, he may as well have been emotionally. Neither Carlos nor I were truly present for him. His father was physically absent, and I, though there in body, was mentally and emotionally distant, lost in the chaos of our lives. Psychologist Allan Schore calls this "proximate separation"—when parents are physically close but emotionally unreachable.

Well-meaning family and friends tried to comfort me with hollow phrases like, "God will provide," and "Every baby is born with a loaf of bread under their arm," but their words did little to ease the weight I felt in my heart. They couldn't understand the inner turmoil I was going through, the guilt of bringing another child into a life already so fraught with instability.

CHAPTER 10

"I felt like a hole in the ground where everything, a phone, a car, a person, could fall in and never be seen again. I wanted to tell someone…but I was too shocked by my own feelings of desolation to speak."

– Sylvia Plath, The Bell Jar

One cold January morning in 1990, as I sat breastfeeding Danny, the doorbell rang furiously, jolting me out of a fragile sense of peace. Before I could unhook Danny and answer it, the door was violently kicked open by the police. We were being evicted. I had no idea this was coming, but in typical fashion, Carlos had been hiding the truth from me for months—he hadn't paid the rent. In what felt like the blink of an eye, our entire world was turned upside down. Our furniture, clothes, and belongings were thrown onto the street, discarded like worthless debris. The neighbors watched the spectacle unfold, their faces a mixture of pity and satisfaction, as though they were witnessing a car crash in slow motion. One neighbor, with a show of shallow sympathy, offered to rent a truck to help us move our things.

We had no choice but to go to my parents' house. As much as I dreaded the judgment I knew awaited me, it was the only place we could turn. My father wasted no time unleashing his fury—recriminations, accusations, and a relentless stream of "I told you so." There were arguments, screaming matches, and words meant to wound, to remind me of how deeply I had failed. Defeated, I retreated to my sister's room, cradling Danny in my arms, the only thing that gave me solace. As night fell and I fed him once more, he was blissfully unaware of the chaos, smiling up at me with innocent eyes, gripping my finger with his tiny hand. In those moments, he was my only anchor.

Carlos didn't last long at my parents' house. Within a month, my father had kicked him out. Carlos went to his parents' home at first, but soon enough, the usual pattern repeated itself. Unable to face reality, Carlos fled, this time to his brother's house in South Bend, Indiana, leaving me and the children behind.

Living with my parents at "Las Moras," a sprawling property my father had recently purchased on the outskirts of the city, was a torment I could never have imagined. Any hope for compassion or support vanished almost immediately. Instead of a home filled with love and understanding, I found myself surrounded by hostility. My father's aggression, once aimed solely at my mother, now extended to all of us. Each morning began with his explosive tirades, loud and merciless, over the most trivial or imagined infractions, casting a shadow over the entire day.

I felt utterly trapped. My marriage to Carlos was beyond repair, yet I couldn't bring myself to leave. With three children and no job, I was completely dependent on my parents, with no clear path forward. Despite his professional and financial success, my father refused to offer me even the smallest help. I had no money for essentials—not even formula for my youngest, Danny. It was my grandfather, well into his seventies and living off a modest pension, who stepped in once again to buy what I could not. My aunt Thelma helped with school supplies, and my sister-in-law Carla, burdened with six children of her own, found ways to lend a hand. While their kindness filled me with gratitude, it also left me drowning in shame for my inability to provide for my own family.

The weight of my father's selfishness and cruel indifference pressed down on me daily. My mother, though present, was powerless, unable to stand up to him even if she wanted to. I was left to navigate this desolate existence alone, caught between my father's rage, my husband's absence, and my own helplessness. Days blurred together in an unending cycle of despair, and though I longed for escape, I could see no way out. My children, with their innocence and light, were my only solace in a world that felt overwhelmingly dark and suffocating.

CHAPTER 11

"For you, a thousand times over."

- Khaled Hosseini, "The Kite Runner"

On December 17, 1990, Canche turned 14 and there wasn't a birthday celebration nor birthday presents as the four of us boarded a plane at La Aurora International Airport in Guatemala City, bound for O'Hare International Airport in Chicago, Illinois. Our ultimate destination was South Bend, Indiana. The internal battle of whether I should stay or go had already been decided for me—there was no choice left. My parent's complete lack of support left me with no other option but to follow my husband to this new "promised land." It wasn't conviction that propelled me forward; it was fear and desperation. Yet, I was resolute in one thing: my children deserved a stable home, food on the table, and, above all, the chance to start each day in peace and love. No more waking up to the screams and chaos that had become routine in my parents' oppressive household. Nor being looked upon by everyone with so much pity and judgment in their eyes as these "poor people."

We landed in South Bend in the early hours of December 18, 1990. This would be our home for the next several decades, a place where our lives would unfold.

South Bend was a place of immense warmth and generosity. Many of its residents welcomed us with open arms, offering kindness and assistance to our newly arrived family. That support became a lifeline during those early years, as we navigated the daunting reality of starting over in a foreign land.

Our most immediate challenge was our immigration status. We had all entered the U.S. on tourist visas, and when those extensions expired, we were left in legal limbo. Neither Carlos nor I could secure legitimate employment without proper documentation, and fear of deportation loomed large over our heads. It was during this uncertain time that Carlos met a priest from the University of Notre Dame who was studying immigration law. Through him, we learned about a newly formed legal aid clinic, led by two remarkable female attorneys who were also faculty members of the university. The clinic had been established to address the growing needs of the Hispanic population in the Michiana area, providing legal support to those seeking a pathway to citizenship.

Our lead counsel, Barbara Szweda, became far more than just our attorney—she became a close, trusted friend, someone I affectionately referred to as a "sister-friend." Barbara was a brilliant legal mind, deeply knowledgeable in immigration law, and passionately committed to helping us secure political asylum. Her dedication to our case was unwavering, as she not only navigated the complexities of our asylum application but also helped us work toward permanent residency and, ultimately, citizenship.

Even though we weren't fleeing Guatemala due to political persecution, Barbara explained how the labyrinth of immigration laws posed an almost insurmountable challenge. These laws were a constantly shifting web, frequently modified to reduce the number of immigrants "allowed" to enter the country. There was no clause to apply for permanent residency based on financial insecurity, which was our true reality. Ironically, the only viable path available to us was to claim political asylum—an option influenced by the U.S.'s deep involvement in the political affairs of Central America, particularly in Guatemala and El Salvador at the time.

I often reflect on how incredibly blessed we were to cross paths with the priest from Notre Dame and with Barbara, an extraordinary, empathetic soul who listened to our story and extended her humanity to help us navigate the complex process of securing our immigration status. Their assistance was a rare gift, something that thousands of immigrants entering this country never experience.

Most who cross the border do so under dangerous circumstances, arriving with little more than the clothes on their backs and no safety net to guide them. They often face a system that seems designed to turn them away, despite the fact that this country was built on the very foundation of welcoming immigrants in search of safety, dignity, and the opportunity to build a better future. These are people who don't want handouts—they are willing to work tirelessly to earn their place.

Immigrants like us all share a common heartbreak: the sorrow of leaving our homeland, our families, and everything familiar in pursuit of a chance to live safely and build a better life. We don't come here to take advantage of anyone or to enjoy a luxury vacation. We come seeking a decent life—something so basic and essential that it should never feel out of reach.

Our journey represents the universal immigrant story, a testament to resilience and hope in the face of overwhelming odds. While we were fortunate to find a lifeline in people who saw our humanity, many others face a lonely, uphill battle. Still, the goal remains the same for all: the right to live, to work, and to create a future free from fear.

The process was long and fraught with uncertainty, but Barbara's guidance and the support we received from the Notre

Dame community provided a glimmer of hope during a time of immense hardship. While South Bend may not have been the thriving town it once was, it became the backdrop for a pivotal chapter in our lives—a place where we found both struggle and sanctuary, where we built a new life in the shadow of the university, and where the seeds of our future were planted in the soil of survival and resilience.

Life took a pivotal turn once we gained legal status in the country that had gradually become our "home." The sense of stability we'd longed for was finally within reach, and with it came the possibility of real progress. Carlos and I wasted no time updating our résumés, eager to find opportunities through the local employment agency. Word spread quickly in South Bend about the new bilingual couple in town, and soon, job offers began to flood in. Working outside the home for me was no longer just an option; it became an absolute necessity to support our growing family.

By this time, my youngest sister, Myriam, had also come to live with us. She had fled Guatemala not to escape war or political strife, but to seek refuge from the emotional tyranny of our own father. Her journey, though different from mine, was equally painful, marked by the need to find safety from the suffocating atmosphere at home. Not long after Myriam left, my mother followed suit. Though she and my father never officially divorced, she had reached her limit, and the weight of their dysfunctional marriage finally pushed her to leave. She followed Myriam to the States, seeking her own version of peace, leaving behind my other young sister, Ginna, who remained in Guatemala, as well as my brother, who had already married and started his own family.

Mom's arrival in South Bend was a bittersweet relief for me. While the fractured state of our family weighed heavily on my heart, I couldn't deny the overwhelming gratitude I felt for her presence. With Mom around, I no longer had to fear the dreaded prospect of sending Danny to daycare, a place I had always imagined to be cold and impersonal. Instead, I could go to work with a calm mind, knowing that Danny was in loving hands, being cared for by someone who truly adored him. Mom took over the household, helping to maintain a sense of stability amid the chaos of our rapidly shifting lives. Her presence was a much-needed lifeline that allowed me to work full-time without constantly worrying about my youngest child's wellbeing.

This arrangement gave me the freedom to focus on my career, something I had longed to do but had been unable to pursue while juggling the demands of motherhood. With Danny safely cared for, I was able to step into the working world, a realm I hadn't fully entered before. The relief I felt knowing he was at home with my mother was immeasurable. Yet, even as life seemed to settle into a new routine, I couldn't shake the sense that the fractures in our family, though temporarily hidden, were still very much present, waiting to surface at any moment.

With that newfound support, I was able to accept my first full-time, well-paying job, complete with benefits. It was 1994, and for the first time since arriving in the U.S., we were starting to feel like we had solid footing. South Bend even began to feel like a nurturing place where we could truly rebuild our lives. We moved into a home we proudly purchased through an incredible program sponsored by St. Joseph County and "La Casa de Amistad," a local non-profit that served the growing Hispanic community. The program allowed us to become homeowners, provided we completed a series of home ownership classes and qualified for a mortgage. We did both. Check and check!

For a time, everything seemed to fall into place. We gave our best efforts, trying hard to establish a sense of normalcy and stability. But even as we checked the boxes of what society defined as success, the unresolved trauma and dysfunction that had plagued our lives continued to cast a shadow over our progress.

Life became a relentless grind—a never-ending cycle of work upon work. As a bilingual professional, I was in high demand, jumping from one job to another, rapidly absorbing everything there was to learn about the corporate world. My résumé grew impressive, and job interviews became routine—I landed every position I pursued. Yet, I never stayed anywhere for long. Sometimes, I would leave the position after only a few months.

Why? Two reasons: first, there was always a better opportunity on the horizon, and second, I could never quite shake the discomfort I felt in these workplaces. Most of my roles were rooted in the health insurance industry, a field riddled with dysfunction, where profits seemed to trump every other priority—including the health and well-being of the people the industry was meant to serve.

At first, my bilingual skills placed me in customer service, where I handled a relentless stream of calls. These weren't just customers—they were human beings in crisis, distressed not only by illness or life-threatening situations but also by the crushing weight of denied claims. These were people who had faithfully paid their premiums, only to find themselves abandoned in their moment of greatest need. It was heartbreaking.

Every call was a plea for help, but instead of solutions, the system offered excuses, red tape, and indifference. As an empath, the daily barrage of despair made me feel physically ill. I could no longer endure the heartache of hearing these stories without being able to make a meaningful difference. As soon as an opportunity arose, I transitioned to roles supporting healthcare providers instead, believing I could help from the other side of the equation.

But what I found was just as disheartening. The compassionate doctors and nurses who had dedicated their lives to healing were trapped in a system that valued efficiency over empathy. Their every decision was scrutinized under the cold lens of profitability. The very people who had chosen this noble profession were being crushed under the weight of inhumane standards, forced to prioritize paperwork and quotas over patient care just to secure reimbursements from the same insurance companies that were failing their patients.

What I had witnessed wasn't just dysfunction—it was a fundamental lack of humanity. The health insurance industry was less about health and more about balancing the books, leaving everyone—patients, providers, and even employees like me—struggling to navigate a system devoid of compassion.

This cycle continued for some time, until one day, an opportunity at Indiana University South Bend's Ernestine Raclin School of the Arts came my way.

The position was for "secretary to the Dean" of the School of the Arts. The title "secretary" may sound outdated now, but back then, it was a coveted role, especially when working for someone as kind and compassionate as Dean Tom Miller. He was one of the most remarkable people I've ever had the pleasure of working with. I was hired in the spring of 2002, and I stayed on as secretary to the Dean until the winter of 2009.

Those were the best professional years of my life. I became the heart of the school and was well-regarded by both the faculty and staff. I took pride in my work and cherished my role, not just as an assistant but as a key figure in the daily operations of the entire department. As time went on, I became more than just a secretary—I was essentially running the school from my desk, especially during the difficult period when Dean Miller's health began to decline.

Tom was diagnosed with Alzheimer's disease, and I did my best to shield him during the early stages of his illness. At first, no one could understand why he was forgetting important dates, losing track of meetings, or even missing classes. It was heartbreaking to watch him slip away slowly, and eventually, the school had to begin the search for a new dean. During this transition period, I was the de facto leader of the Raclin School of the Arts. While the administration searched for Tom's replacement, I took on the responsibility of managing the school's day-to-day affairs. Those years were a bittersweet blend of professional fulfillment and personal loss.

During this time, my mother and younger sister had come and gone from our household, their stay had offered moments of comfort while also underscoring the fractured state of our family. Our oldest son, seeking independence and a fresh start, moved out. He first settled in San Diego, California, before eventually making Chicago his home—a city that would define the next two decades of his life. There, he thrived, creating a life far removed from the turbulence of our family dynamics.

Amid the challenges of that period, a true source of joy arrived on July 16, 2002, with the birth of our grandson, Ethan. His presence was a radiant light, bringing pure and unfiltered happiness to all of us. He ignited a spark of hope and love that helped us endure the difficulties we faced. My daughter, following a pattern familiar to the women in our family, experienced a whirlwind romance that led to an unexpected pregnancy. Soon after, she and Kenny married and began navigating the complexities of building a life together. Their journey, however, was fraught with challenges and uncertainty.

The shadow of 9/11 loomed large in the collective consciousness of the nation. The fear and vulnerability brought on by those unprecedented attacks lingered, shaping the mood of the era. In many ways, it felt like their generational equivalent of the 1976 earthquake—a defining existential moment for Carlos and me—leaving a mark on their lives and decisions.

*"Our grandson, Ethan Ezra Nicodemus
Baldizon, born on July 16, 2002"*

Kenny, feeling the weight of responsibility as a new father, made the difficult decision to re-enlist in the military.

He was quickly sent to Germany for training and soon deployed to Iraq as an Army soldier. My daughter, who was left with the overwhelming task of raising Ethan, moved into a house right across the street from us. She, too, had to grow up fast—far quicker than any of us had anticipated. It was a familiar story, one that echoed my own struggles when I was her age. But instead of staying close, she made the heart-wrenching decision to join Kenny in Germany. She chose to reside on a military base during a time of war. It was a decision I understood, but it didn't make it any less painful for me. She was fleeing from the dysfunction and chaos of our family, a reality she could no longer tolerate.

"Beba and Ethan in Europe"

When they left, the pain was unbearable, as though I were mourning a death. The absence of Ethan's laughter filled the house with an oppressive emptiness, and I found myself spiraling into a deep well of loneliness and despair. Grief consumed me, and I turned to the one constant that had always numbed my pain—vodka. I withdrew into the bottle, seeking solace in its oblivion, with no will or desire to climb out. The consequences of my drinking were steep, but I was too broken to care.

The house grew quieter still, the lack of children to care for amplifying the silence. Only Danny remained, just starting high school, and he was caught in the unspoken tension of a marriage unraveling. Carlos and I were locked in a cold war—years of resentment, mistrust, and unspoken grievances boiling beneath the surface. Though I had always stepped in to stabilize our family, compensating for Carlos' inability to hold a job or provide support, his escalating paranoia and unfounded accusations of infidelity became unbearable. His obsessive need to control every aspect of my life suffocated me, demanding my complete attention and isolating me from any semblance of freedom or happiness.

By the time I reached my forties, I realized how much of myself I had lost. At work, I was confident and respected—a professional at the top of her game. But at home, I was a shadow of that person, diminished into submission by years of unmet needs and oppressive control. I felt like an empty nester before my children had even fully left, haunted by a loneliness that seemed to echo through every part of my life. I longed for more—more meaning, more purpose, and above all, more respect.

Carlos often claimed to love me, but his overwhelming insecurities and possessiveness eroded the foundation of our marriage. His attempts to keep me tethered to him unraveled any possibility of growth or connection. By the time our relationship ended, I saw clearly how much of myself I had sacrificed to maintain the fragile illusion of stability. Staying silent, lowering my head, and enduring had cost me too much.

Those years were some of the darkest. Drinking, which had started as a way to cope, quickly became a daily crutch. My destructive lifestyle—excessive drinking, poor eating habits, and heavy smoking—took over. I stopped caring for myself entirely, drifting without a spiritual anchor or a sense of purpose. My disconnection from the Catholic Church left me yearning for something deeper, a source of authentic inspiration.

My life became a double-edged existence. At work, I functioned, excelled even, masking the hollow, broken version of myself that existed outside the office. At home, I lived mechanically—waking up, working, drinking, smoking, and sleeping in a monotonous cycle that felt devoid of meaning or joy. It was a soulless existence, one I convinced myself was all I deserved.

The worst part was the resignation. I believed this was the life I was meant for—that the numbness, the self-destruction, and the isolation were my lot. Trapped in a cycle of despair, I felt as though I had disappeared entirely, a hollow shell drowning in my own helplessness with no end in sight.

CHAPTER 12

"In a world of tension and breakdown it is necessary for there to be those who seek to integrate their inner lives not by avoiding anguish and running away from problems, but by facing them in their naked reality and in their ordinariness."

– Thomas Merton

Then, one day while I was at work, I received an instant message from my sister, Myriam, who was back in Guatemala by then. The news was devastating: our father had suffered a stroke. Though he survived, it left him paralyzed on one side of his body, weak and vulnerable. The reality of it hit me hard, and I knew I had to return home to Guatemala to see him. Yet, the trip was not as easy to arrange as I had hoped. Carlos, who hadn't set foot in Guatemala since we left in 1990, was gripped by fear at the very thought of going back. His terror, compounded by his deep distrust of me and his pathological jealousy, made the prospect of traveling without him unbearable. I knew that if I went alone, I'd pay a steep emotional price. I had, afterall, gone through this experience before when in years past I had "dared" to travel to Guatemala without him. During my absence he went crazy and went through all my private things, including my journal, where he used the powers of his sick imagination to prove that I was having an affair with a Notre Dame priest I had befriended. He made my life miserable while I was visiting my family, tracking my every move, locating me and calling me wherever I happened to be - an impressive feat in the era prior to cell phones. Upon my return I found a lunatic embodied in the shell of a man...and I paid dearly.

Reluctantly, I delayed our departure until Carlos was ready to travel, hoping we would still make it in time for my father's 70th birthday on February 27th. Another concern lingered in the back of my mind—Danny. He was a sophomore in high school, and this would be the first time I'd be leaving him behind without any siblings to watch over him. Fortunately, a trusted neighbor, the mother of Danny's best friend, promised to keep an eye on him while we were away.

As we packed the car to travel to take our flight from O'Hare, I was in the middle of giving our neighbor all the contact information she might need when Danny handed me the phone. My heart sank as I heard the words on the other end. I was too late. My father had passed away at 4 a.m. that morning, just hours before we were set to arrive in Guatemala. The opportunity to see him one last time, to hug him, to say the things I'd left unsaid, was gone forever.

It felt as though the Universe had delivered a cruel blow, and I was left reeling from the timing of it all. We arrived in Guatemala City at 6 a.m. on February 23rd, and by 3 p.m., my father was buried. The sight of him lying so peacefully in his coffin was both heart-wrenching and surreal. He looked so young, so serene, so handsome. Burying my father was one of the most traumatic experiences of my life. Our relationship had always been fraught, weighed down by his alcoholism, his abusive treatment of all of us, and the bitter animosity he harbored toward Carlos. Despite all of that, I had wanted to return to celebrate his birthday, to show him pictures of his great-grandchild, and simply to say, "I love you." Now, I'd never get the chance.

When we returned to South Bend, I was still deep in the throes of grief.

I sank deeper into a relentless cycle of self-loathing, feeling as though I had completely failed in every important role I had ever held. In my own mind, I was a disgrace. I had gotten pregnant at 17, tarnishing my family's reputation, and as a wife, I seemed to have fueled my husband's obsessive jealousy. Worse, as a mother, I had somehow driven my daughter away—both physically and emotionally—into a war zone's chaos. The guilt from these failures consumed me.

As my self-hatred deepened, so did my feelings for Carlos. What had once been love vanished not over time but all at once, like the flick of a switch. It wasn't that he changed into someone else—it became clear that perhaps he had always been the narrow-minded man I now saw before me. My tolerance for his suffocating presence, once held together by fragile civility, had shattered. Our home was now a silent battlefield, much like my parents' house had been, except this war was quiet but no less destructive. Every moment with him felt like a confrontation, even without words.

I came to realize that my meekness had been my downfall. My fear of conflict, my desire to "keep the peace" at all costs, had cost me so much more. By yielding to his control, by allowing his jealousy to dictate my every move, I had lost the most precious chance of all—the opportunity to reconcile with my father before he passed away. I couldn't undo it, couldn't reverse the consequences of my silence. That moment was gone forever. I began to wonder what else I might lose if I continued to sacrifice myself for Carlos' comfort. Would I lose my dignity? My soul? How far would I go to keep him content, and how much more of myself would I have to destroy in the process?

CHAPTER 13

"And the day came when the risk to remain tight in a bud was more painful than the risk it took to blossom."

- Anais Nin

In January 2008, a pivotal moment arrived that marked the beginning of my path toward freedom. Carlos and I had an altercation that, while deeply humiliating, would become the final straw. His unchecked jealousy reached new heights that day, and he disrespected me in front of our sons. That public humiliation was more than I could bear. In that moment, I made an irreversible decision: I would never again share a marital bed with the man who had been my husband for more than half my life.

After the incident, I sought refuge in the solitude of my home. I retreated to a small room in the basement, a space originally meant for our youngest child when the house had been full of life. Now, it became my sanctuary, a place where I could begin the slow process of self-reflection and healing. In that confined room, I embarked on an inward journey, seeking clarity and meaning in a life that had become so distorted by fear, jealousy, and resentment.

It was during this period of isolation that an unexpected series of events began to unfold. One of the most profound was the introduction of Eckhart Tolle's work into my life. His book *"A New Earth: Awakening to Your Life's Purpose"*, which followed the success of *"The Power of Now"*, became a beacon of hope for me. I began to see beyond the external circumstances of my life and delve into the deeper dimensions of my being. Tolle's words resonated deeply, offering me a glimpse of my true self—the part of me that had been buried under years of suppression and self-doubt. It was as though I had been waiting for this message my whole life, and finally, the teacher had appeared.

As the Buddha wisely said, "When the student is ready, the teacher will appear." In the quiet of that basement room, I began to discover a new source of strength within myself. I embarked on a journey of self-love and self-acceptance, finally starting to reclaim the life I was meant to live. I realized that my life's purpose wasn't something outside of me; it was something that had been within me all along, waiting to be awakened.

By the summer of 2008, I took the most decisive step yet—I filed for divorce. Carlos, however, refused to leave the house, forcing me out of the basement and into a small, modest apartment. It was the first time in my entire life that I had lived alone, and while the newfound independence brought fear and uncertainty, it also opened up a path to freedom. My days were spent going to work and returning to a quiet, empty apartment—one that echoed with loneliness but also with the possibilities of a new beginning. The silence was a stark contrast to the chaos I had lived through, and in that emptiness, I found room to confront my deepest fears, including one that had haunted me for years: driving.

For so long, the idea of getting behind the wheel terrified me. But if I was truly going to reclaim my life, I knew I had to face that fear head-on. I enrolled in driving school, and although my first attempt at attaining my driver's license test ended in failure, I didn't give up. With persistence, I eventually earned my first—and only—driver's license from the State of Indiana at the age of 51. That small piece of plastic was more than just a license to drive; it symbolized my growing autonomy and determination to forge a new path for myself.

It was such an accomplishment in my life that even my trusted childhood friends, Anaite and Maya, traveled to South Bend to see me and celebrate this momentous occasion. What a hoot! It was not only the license they came to celebrate but also that I had finally taken the step towards a life of dignity and self-respect.

Meanwhile, the divorce proceedings dragged on, with Carlos making things difficult at every turn. He requested that I relinquish my rights to the house if I wanted the divorce to go through. Despite my attorney's advice to fight for what was legally mine, I chose to let it go. I didn't want possessions; I wanted peace, freedom, and the chance to live my life on my own terms. Material things no longer mattered to me—I was ready to move forward.

Around this time, another synchronicity appeared in my life, because although I had a driver's license I still had no car to drive. A friend from the theater department at IUSB—a belly-dancing professor, no less—gifted me her beloved 1989 Mercedes-Benz. The car, a faded red "baby" Mercedes, was well-worn but reliable, and it became the first and only car I've ever owned. The gesture felt like something out of Janis Joplin's famous song, *"Oh Lord, won't you buy me a Mercedes-Benz?"* In a way, it was as if the universe had answered my unspoken call.

"My first and only driver's license (obtained at 51 years old) and my red 1989 baby Mercedes Benz, first and only car ever owned"

But even though the car held sentimental value, when I was offered a new job in Chicago, I gave the car away to a young man who had just become a father and needed it for work. It felt like the right thing to do, a way to pay it forward as I continued to embrace the principles of letting go and creating space for new possibilities in my life.

The job offer that drew me to Chicago seemed almost fated, another synchronicity in a growing chain of events that pointed me toward a brighter future. I had applied for a position of Department Coordinator at the Department of Interactive Arts and Media at Columbia College Chicago. When I sat down for the interview, it was as if the universe had perfectly aligned my past experiences with the role they needed filled. My time as Secretary to the Dean of the School of the Arts at IUSB had prepared me in ways I couldn't have foreseen, and the department chair I was interviewing with seemed to recognize that instantly. By the time the interview ended, I felt a sense of certainty that this position was mine to fill.

As I walked out of the building and into the bustling streets of Chicago, I knew that I was stepping into a new chapter of my life. The city, with all its energy and possibility, felt like a fresh start. With each step, I left behind the shackles of my past and embraced a future full of promise, purpose, and newfound freedom.

On a cold Monday morning in January 2010, I walked into 916 S. Wabash, my new workplace. Everything felt different, even my name, now I was Blanca Martini, a name imbued with elegance and the mystery of a James Bond heroine. It suited me perfectly. The sophistication and allure that the name carried resonated with the woman I was becoming, and in this vibrant, cosmopolitan city, I was determined to create a life that would reflect the freedom I had fought so hard to gain.

The cost of my new life had been high—sacrificing my home, a 32 year marriage, and nearly every connection to my former self. But I had no regrets. Each loss had been a necessary step toward liberation, and now, in Chicago, I would make every sacrifice worthwhile. I embraced the lifestyle of a true Chicagoan with open arms, reveling in the fact that for the first time, I didn't need a car to get around. The L train and CTA buses became my trusted means of transportation, taking me wherever I needed to go in the sprawling metropolis. The city's pulse became my own, and soon I found myself with a circle of new friends and even a few boyfriends—an ironic twist given the years Carlos had spent consumed by jealousy. The affairs he had once imagined finally materialized, but only after I had fully reclaimed my independence.

Yet despite the allure of romantic adventures, I knew that a relationship was not the path I was seeking. After everything I had endured, I wasn't about to surrender my hard-won freedom for anyone, no matter how tempting. This was a time for me— to evolve, to grow, and to discover who I truly was. It was as if I was finally giving birth to a mature psyche, one that had always longed to break free but had been stifled for so long. In this new chapter of my life, I was focused on something far greater than fleeting relationships: I was focused on myself, my growth, and my journey toward becoming a strong, independent woman.

Chicago became the perfect backdrop for this transformation. It was a city of infinite possibilities, a place where I could pursue the wisdom and knowledge I had always craved but never had the chance to fully explore. The teachings of Gary Zukav and my beloved Eckhart Tolle were just the beginning. Their insights had laid the foundation, but there was so much more to discover—so many other voices, philosophies, and ideas that beckoned me. The city became my playground for intellectual and spiritual growth, a place where I could immerse myself in learning and expanding.

This city—this life—was my rebirth. Chicago offered the perfect environment for me to shed the limitations of the past and step into a future of my own making. It was here that I would finally live the life I had long dreamed of, unbound by the constraints of my former self, ready to embrace the world with open arms. Blanca Martini had arrived.

CHAPTER 14

"Know Thyself and to Thyself Be True"

Early in my time at Columbia College Chicago, I often took lunch breaks to explore the neighborhood around me. One day, I wandered upon a small park and the historic Dearborn Station. The station, with its stately red brick exterior and towering clock standing over 200 feet high, had been restored to its former glory. Once a bustling hub for intercity travel in the late 1800s, Dearborn Station had now become an architectural gem of the city, and this charming area quickly became my favorite place to visit.

It was during one of these strolls that I stumbled upon a place that would forever change my life: Equilibrium Energy Education, affectionately known as e3. A small but inviting storefront caught my eye with its display of mesmerizing crystals, and a sign in the window that read, "10-minute lunch meditation." Up until that moment, meditation had always seemed like something reserved for monks or spiritual masters, far beyond my reach. But there was a voice inside me urging me to take the plunge, and so, driven by curiosity, I stepped inside.

That 10-minute guided meditation, led by the owner herself, was nothing short of a revelation. The session was gentle yet transformative, leaving me with a profound sense of peace and clarity that I hadn't experienced before. As I emerged from the meditation, the owner kindly gave me a tour of the space, explaining the array of workshops, seminars, and events designed for personal growth and spiritual evolution. It was as though I had found a hidden treasure—a beautiful synchronicity placed perfectly on my path.

From that moment on, e3 became a sanctuary for me. The workshops and book clubs I attended opened my heart and mind, ushering me into a deeper understanding of myself. I became an "Angel Member," joining a community of like-minded individuals also on their spiritual journeys. In this nurturing environment, I began to flourish.

My journey toward self-discovery and personal freedom was marked by yet another milestone in April of 2014: I became a United States citizen. This wasn't just a change of nationality—it felt like a rebirth, a formal acknowledgment of the new identity I had worked so hard to claim. Becoming a citizen symbolized the full embrace of my independence and the life I was carving out for myself in Chicago.

Around this time, I found myself devouring books on spirituality, Buddhism, and mindfulness. Jon Kabat-Zinn's work on Mindfulness-Based Stress Reduction (MBSR) particularly resonated with me. His teachings offered a practical, accessible way to integrate mindfulness into everyday life, and as fate would have it, an MBSR course was being offered at The Insight Center in downtown Chicago, led by Dr. Chris Chroniak. Thanks to a timely income tax refund—my first since the divorce—I eagerly signed up for the course.

The experience was transformative. The MBSR course was more than just stress reduction—it was a profound journey into mindful living. Through meditation, somatic exercises, and deep discussions, I began to unravel the layers of illusion that had clouded my perception for so long. Day by day, I felt the weight of old burdens lift as I embraced the practice of mindfulness. My world seemed to expand, revealing a vibrant reality that had always been there, but which I had been too preoccupied to notice. I was living in Chicago as an independent woman, and it was exhilarating.

I felt a deep hunger for more—more spiritual growth, more knowledge, more life. Chicago had become the fertile ground for my personal evolution, and I was determined to cultivate everything it had to offer.

At work, I enjoyed my role in the Interactive Arts Department, even though it was an environment dominated by the tech-savvy, mostly male students who spent hours engrossed in video games. The U.S. Army even awarded the department a $1.5 million grant to develop a video game focusing on eye coordination. Despite this, the department chair, a progressive and visionary woman, sought to push the boundaries. She wanted to create games with a purpose, focusing on environmental consciousness and inviting more women into the field. I admired her courage and drive, seeing in her a reflection of my own quest for growth and freedom.

However, her vision faced immense resistance. The tech community, as well as many of the male faculty members and upper administration, ridiculed her for trying to shift the industry's focus. Yet, despite their contempt, she pressed forward, balancing her role as an artist, department chair, and caregiver to her family—including a spouse confined to a wheelchair after a tragic accident.

It was disheartening to witness the immense pressures she faced. In a world where men often had someone else to care for their basic needs, allowing them to pursue their ambitions freely, women like her—and like many of us—shouldered the heavy burden of balancing caregiving with professional responsibilities. The dream of equality that the Women's Liberation Movement had promised still felt distant. We are still living in a man's world.

Eventually, the relentless stress took its toll on her health, leading to a diagnosis of breast cancer. At first, only a few of us were aware, but as her condition worsened, it became evident to everyone. The weight of her professional and personal obligations had become too much, and she took a one-year sabbatical to focus on her recovery.

During her absence, an interim chair was appointed—a man from the music department who had little understanding of or alignment with the vision of the Interactive Arts Department. Under his leadership, the department transformed into a "man cave," where the techies now roamed free, unchecked. The progressive vision that had once given the department its innovative edge dissolved into a sea of masculine bravado.

I went to work each day, hoping for the return of the true leader who had inspired me, but the news that her sabbatical would become permanent was a devastating blow. The final straw came when the interim chair was officially appointed to the role. I couldn't stand to stay in an environment that had become toxic with misogyny. Without a safety net or backup plan, I did what I had to do—I quit.

Walking away from the highest-paying job I'd ever had was terrifying, but I knew I couldn't sacrifice my values. Just as I had left my marriage with nothing but my dignity and freedom, I left this job in search of something truer to my spirit. But now, the stakes were higher. I was living in one of the most expensive cities in the country, and the reality of my decision hit hard. Panic set in as I scrambled to find work, applying to every job I could, hoping for a lifeline in this bold new chapter of my life.

Eventually, I landed a job at Northwestern University, working in the Registrar's office within the Transcript department. On the surface, this seemed like a prestigious and exciting opportunity. After all, Northwestern is one of the most esteemed academic institutions in Illinois, and its name is recognized globally. Yet, on my very first day, as I made my way home, I found myself unexpectedly in tears. The sense of disappointment that washed over me was overwhelming. How could I feel so disillusioned? I was working at the pinnacle of the academic world in my region, a place that symbolizes honor, respect, and success. And yet, despite the prestigious name, the reality of the job felt hollow, far removed from the aspirations that had once driven me.

The excitement I had hoped to feel was quickly dampened by the mundane nature of the work. The work offered no challenge, no creative outlet, and no opportunity to apply the knowledge I had worked so hard to gain. It was the very definition of a "paper-pushing" job, and it left me feeling empty, unappreciated, and disconnected from my deeper ambitions. The only silver lining was the paycheck and the promise of good benefits, though even those felt like hollow consolations in the face of such professional dissatisfaction.

Still, I wasn't willing to give in to despair. Determined to make the most of the situation, I focused on one of the more valuable perks the job offered—tuition assistance. I had already utilized a similar benefit at Columbia College Chicago when Danny pursued his Bachelor of Arts degree, and now it was my turn. This opportunity became my lifeline, a way to turn an otherwise unfulfilling situation into a stepping stone toward something greater.

I enrolled in Northwestern's Professional Services Department to pursue a certificate in Nonprofit Management and Philanthropy. This decision felt like the rekindling of a lost purpose, a way to redirect my energy toward something meaningful. The coursework was challenging, stimulating, and aligned with my growing desire to contribute to causes that mattered. For the first time in a while, I felt a sense of purpose returning to my life.

The program was demanding, but I was determined to see

it through. After three years of dedicated study—balancing work, life, and education—I proudly earned my diploma. That piece of paper represented much more than just the completion of a certificate program; it symbolized resilience, reinvention, and the constant pursuit of growth, even in the face of setbacks.

Northwestern may not have been the prestigious career I had envisioned, but it provided a path for me to reclaim my sense of direction. I walked away from the experience not just with a certificate, but with the knowledge that I could find purpose even in the most unexpected places.

During this transformative period in my life, I discovered a nonprofit organization called Pueblo a Pueblo, located in the town of Panabaj on the shores of Lake Atitlán, Guatemala. This community had suffered tremendously from a devastating landslide during Hurricane Stan in 2005, and years later, it was still grappling with the aftermath. The need for funds to rebuild infrastructure and provide essential services like healthcare, nutrition, and education was urgent, and the cause resonated deeply within me.

Inspired by this newfound passion, I felt a surge of energy and determination. I decided to organize a fundraising event in Chicago to support the recovery efforts in Panabaj. The timing of my first event was particularly fitting; it coincided with the vibrant Pride Parade in June, a celebration that filled the streets with joy and inclusivity.

My apartment, located at the bustling corner of Cornelia and Broadway—right along the parade route—turned out to be the perfect venue for the gathering. Since moving to Chicago, I had forged close friendships within the gay community, a group of men whose warmth and support I cherished. With a prime view of the parade from my corner apartment and being just across the street from Treasure Island, known for its expansive parking lot, I was excited about the possibilities.

I set a modest entry fee for the fundraiser, which included

food and beverages, and encouraged guests to bring their own alcohol. This way, attendees could enjoy the parade from the comfort of my spacious living room, stepping out to join the festivities whenever they pleased—all while contributing to a worthy cause. To add a personal touch, I gifted Guatemalan friendship bracelets to those who donated more than the entry fee, ensuring that everyone left with a brochure detailing how their contributions would directly benefit the people of Panabaj.

The event turned out to be a tremendous success! The combination of a meaningful cause, a prime location, and the lively atmosphere of the Pride Parade created an unforgettable experience. The overwhelming response to that first fundraiser inspired me to host another event the following year, further supporting the recovery efforts in Panabaj.

Through these gatherings, I was not only able to raise much-needed funds but also raise awareness about a cause that was close to my heart. These events became a celebration of community and friendship in a city that had embraced me as my new home.

Energized by this success and brimming with new ideas, I began to take stock of my surroundings. It dawned on me that I was surrounded by artists—starting with my own children, each blessed with unique and remarkable creative talents. This realization ignited a new wave of inspiration within me, prompting me to organize yet another fundraiser. This time, I envisioned an event that would tap into the artistic gifts of those around me.

I reached out to my children, their friends, and my vibrant network of talented individuals I had met over the years. Together, we planned a wine and cheese night at one of my favorite spots—a charming yarn store owned by a friend of a friend. Nestled in a quaint neighborhood, the venue provided just the right amount of space to showcase the donated artwork.

To make the event even more special, we decided to auction the art, allowing guests to bid on each piece and further contribute to the cause.

Once again, the night was a tremendous success! The funds raised this time went to another remarkable nonprofit organization in Panajachel, Lake Atitlán, called "Mayan Families." This organization focused on assisting the indigenous population, particularly in areas related to education—a cause that resonated deeply with my own values. After the fundraiser, I reached out to Sandra, the founder of Mayan Families, to send her the donations. Through our correspondence, I learned about her inspiring journey.

Originally from Australia, Sandra had been visiting Lake Atitlán when Hurricane Stan devastated parts of the region. Moved by the devastation, she and her husband, who hailed from San Diego, quickly mobilized their friends and networks to raise significant funds for recovery efforts. From that initial grassroots response, Mayan Families was born, and for over a decade, the organization had been dedicated to supporting low-income indigenous families.

A few weeks later, I received a heartfelt thank-you card from the children of Mayan Families, accompanied by a beautiful photograph of their smiling faces. Their innocence and hope touched me profoundly, and I printed the picture, hanging it in my cubicle at Northwestern. It became a beacon of light during long days at work, reminding me of a future where I could leave behind the confines of my cubicle to fully dedicate myself to helping children like those bright, beautiful souls.

Months later, a wonderful opportunity arose. My two sons and I traveled to Guatemala to celebrate my mother's 75th birthday, and I was determined to visit Lake Atitlán. Before our arrival, I scheduled a tour of Mayan Families with Sandra, eager to witness firsthand the impactful work being done.

Little did I know that this connection would lead to something even more profound. Eventually, I would become a staff member at Mayan Families, working directly with the children and families who had inspired me so deeply. What had begun as a fundraising effort would evolve into a fulfilling opportunity to actively participate in the meaningful work I had long envisioned.

CHAPTER 15

"Pain is inevitable. Suffering is not. Suffering arises from grasping. Release grasping and be free of suffering."

– principle of Buddhist psychology

By the end of 2015, stress had reached an overwhelming peak, primarily from work, not caused by the mindless work I was performing but due to the combative, hypocritical and down right nasty relationship I had with my direct supervisor. On New Year's Eve, I found myself rushed to the hospital, just like during my pregnancy with Danny, suffering once again from atrial fibrillation. This heart condition, caused by erratic electrical signals, left my heart in an abnormal rhythm for more than 24 hours despite the doctors' best efforts to stabilize it. The situation forced a sobering realization: my body was no longer able to withstand the relentless pressure I had been under. The doctors suggested a minimally invasive procedure called cryoablation to fix the issue, and I began 2016 with a stark wake-up call—my stress had not only consumed my mind but had manifested as a potentially serious heart condition.

In the aftermath, rather than confronting the root of my stress in a healthy way, I fell back into old habits. Once again, I turned to alcohol as a form of self-medication, seeking solace in late-night drinking sessions with a close friend. These nights provided temporary escape but led to humiliating public episodes and mornings thick with guilt. I began to see the damage I was doing—not just to myself but to my youngest son, who had started following the same destructive path. It was a painful reflection of the example I was setting. The realization that I was not only jeopardizing my own health but also his pushed me toward a critical decision: I had to break the cycle. I committed to weekly therapy sessions, a choice that proved to be transformative.

Therapy became the lifeline I so desperately needed, offering clarity in a way that alcohol never could. Week by week, I began to unravel the layers of unresolved issues that had weighed me down for so long. We tackled the pain of my divorce, the upheaval that came with moving to Chicago, and the mounting pressure I faced at work. But the hardest challenge to face was my shifting relationship with my now adult children. For years, I had seen myself only as a mother and caregiver. Suddenly, I had to navigate new dynamics with my children—adults who no longer needed, and sometimes didn't want, my nurturing.

Although I knew I had done my best as a parent, understanding this intellectually did little to soothe the guilt that lingered. I loved my children deeply, but I couldn't escape the awareness that my parenting had been shaped not only by love but also by my own unresolved traumas and the constant stress I had lived with. Therapy helped me recognize that I had coped the best I could with the tools I had at the time, but this knowledge didn't immediately ease the heavy burden of guilt. It clung to me, a constant companion, reminding me of the imperfections in my love and the unintended consequences of my choices.

Learning to manage stress in healthier ways was essential, but it wasn't easy. The effects of years of unchecked stress, from the hospital visit to the emotional damage, underscored how deeply it had infiltrated my life. Therapy became a process of healing, but it also required hard work—work that was slow and emotionally taxing. Confronting the wounds I had long buried was both rewarding and grueling. However, as I delved into the painful realities of my past, I began to see the power of truly addressing the root of my stress. I was no longer relying on temporary fixes like alcohol to numb the pain, but rather, I was building resilience, learning to manage stress in ways that didn't sacrifice my health or well-being.

The key, I realized, was in finding better coping mechanisms. Instead of bottling up emotions or turning to destructive habits, I had to embrace healthier outlets—whether that meant talking through my struggles in therapy, practicing mindfulness, or simply learning to set boundaries at work and in life. These were the tools that allowed me to not only manage stress but to reclaim control over my life.

The journey was slow, and progress wasn't always linear, but it illuminated a path to healing that felt sustainable. Therapy helped me navigate through the darkest moments, but it also required me to put in the effort to heal. It wasn't an easy fix, but it was far more rewarding than anything alcohol could have offered. Most importantly, it showed me that while stress may be inevitable, there are better ways to deal with it—ways that strengthen you, rather than break you down.

This backdrop colored my life in 2016—a year that felt bleak on so many fronts. The political landscape in America had shifted dramatically, leaving many, including myself, feeling unmoored and anxious about the future. It was a challenging year, yet amidst the turmoil, there was one glimmer of hope shining on the horizon: my 40th high school reunion in Guatemala. Forty years have passed? How had the time flown by so swiftly? Though I hadn't officially graduated with the class of '76, I still felt a deep connection to those classmates who had witnessed my entry into adulthood. So, I decided to join the celebration and booked a ticket for a short four-day trip to Guatemala City.

Prior to my short trip on the morning of Friday, October 7th, as I sat at my dining room table, something extraordinary happened. A magnificent Monarch butterfly alighted on the outside of my window, eleven stories up - in the Windy City! For reasons I couldn't fully articulate, I felt the sighting was an omen—a sign, though I wasn't yet sure of what it foretold.

As it turned out, my intuition was spot on. Later that afternoon, I was summoned to a meeting with my boss. Upon entering the Registrar's office, I was met by a table full of individuals from Human Resources waiting for me. My stomach dropped. I was being fired.

The reasons they provided were flimsy, lacking any real justification for such a drastic action. There had been no prior incidents of misconduct, nothing that would have warranted such a harsh decision. I was devastated. The shock hit me like a tidal wave, and I found myself trembling and crying uncontrollably.

In an unexpected moment of kindness, the head of Human Resources, clearly moved by my distress, asked everyone to leave the room. Once we were alone, she gently advised me to file for unemployment—something I had never even considered. Confused, I questioned how I could possibly qualify for benefits when I was being fired for supposed misconduct. She reassured me that she would personally review my application and would not deny it, acknowledging that my termination was, in her view, unfair. Her compassion provided a small comfort amidst the overwhelming turmoil.

On the train ride home, I sat in a daze, repeatedly asking myself, *What had just happened?*

Fear, that unwelcome shadow looming over me once again, surged back with a vengeance. It felt like an old, relentless companion returning to rob me of peace. I was thrown back into the exhausting uncertainty of job searching, a cycle I had hoped was behind me. Would it ever end? The only job that had ever given me genuine fulfillment was at IUSB in South Bend, where I had been respected, valued, and surrounded by colleagues who had become family. But going back to South Bend wasn't an option. I was stuck, grappling with the suffocating anxiety of not knowing where my next steps would lead. The familiar dread of uncertainty began to claw at me again, clouding any semblance of hope.

Life had become a series of relentless curveballs. Every time I thought I had regained my footing, something would knock me off balance. I tried to stay grounded, but the constant upheaval was draining, and the emotional exhaustion took its toll. The idea of finding a place where I could not only survive but thrive seemed further away than ever.

In my late 50s, finding a job became an uphill battle due to ageism. Despite my experience and qualifications, in-person interviews always ended the same way: I was labeled "overqualified"—a thinly veiled rejection based on my age. Each rejection chipped away at my confidence, and as unemployment benefits dwindled, panic set in. The fear of not being able to pay rent became a constant, unsettling reality.

CHAPTER 16

*"The prime purpose in this life is to help others. And
if you can't help them, at least don't hurt them."*

- H.H. Dalai Lama

Just when I thought I had reached a dead end, completely cornered with no way out, my best friend at the time stepped in like a guardian angel. She offered to pay for me to enroll in a 10-week course to earn a TEFL (Teaching English as a Foreign Language) certificate, a gesture that felt like nothing short of a lifeline. In the midst of overwhelming uncertainty, her generosity provided a flicker of hope, something to cling to as I tried to piece together a plan for the future.

The new plan was to return to Guatemala, a decision that had come much sooner than I had originally envisioned. I had always imagined making that move in about four years, after retirement, when I could transition into a more peaceful chapter of my life. But life, with its constant twists and unpredictable turns, had other plans for me. Instead of the leisurely, well-thought-out relocation I had once dreamed of, this move now felt urgent—more a necessity than a choice.

Despite the accelerated timeline, the idea of returning to Guatemala brought a sense of relief. Earning the TEFL certificate, along with the Nonprofit Management certification

I had already acquired, would at least position me to find work in the country. And not just any job—I had long dreamed of settling near Lake Atitlán, that tranquil paradise nestled in the highlands. The thought of waking up each morning to the breathtaking beauty of the lake and the surrounding volcanoes was a vision I had held onto for years. It was a place where I could reconnect with my roots, recharge my spirit, and perhaps, finally, find the peace that had eluded me for so long.

Yet, even as I clung to that vision, I couldn't help but feel a mix of apprehension and excitement. This move wasn't happening under the ideal circumstances I had once imagined. I wasn't retiring into a life of leisure, but rather, diving into a new chapter that required me to keep working, to rebuild myself yet again. There were no guarantees, no certainty that this plan would work out as I hoped. But after years of struggling to stay afloat, it felt like a necessary leap of faith.

Even as I made the decision, a heavy weight settled in my heart. The most difficult part of this transition would be the inevitable separation from my children. I understood, logically, that this was the right move for me, but emotionally, the thought of leaving them behind was excruciating.

"Last Thanksgiving spent in Chicago with all my children in 2016"

Despite the internal conflict, I pressed forward, driven by the belief that this new path held the promise of fulfillment. After completing my TEFL certification, things began to fall into place faster than I expected. I managed to secure a place to live—an AirB&B in Panajachel, the main town on the shores of Lake Atitlán. I figured that once I was settled there, I would reconnect with Sandra from Mayan Families, the nonprofit I had supported in the past. I hoped that through her, I could find a position within the organization and begin to make a real difference in the lives of the local community.

I arrived in Panajachel with a sense of cautious optimism. The lush landscapes and the serene waters of Lake Atitlán welcomed me, filling me with a sense of peace. Though the future was still uncertain, there was a small flicker of hope. If I could land a position with Mayan Families, I believed I could rebuild my life with purpose and intention. My journey wasn't over—it was just beginning again, in a place that felt like it had been waiting for me all along.

But...

Life in Panajachel (Pana) turned out to be far from the serene refuge I had once known. Although I was surrounded by the breathtaking beauty of Lake Atitlán, the town itself had evolved dramatically since my last memories of it in the '70s. Back then, Pana was a sleepy, idyllic village, a haven for hippies like me, drawn to its promise of peace, love, and simplicity. But the Pana I returned to was unrecognizable—now a bustling, noisy hub at the heart of the region.

What had once been a quiet escape had transformed into the "Manhattan of Lake Atitlán," as I jokingly began to call it. Pana had become the nerve center for business, banking, and commerce in the area. All legal transactions, transportation, and communication routes funneled through the town, making it a vital link between the surrounding villages and the capital city. The tranquil mornings I had longed for were instead filled with the harsh sounds of busy traffic, the buzzing of tuc-tucs—those small, three-wheeled motorized rickshaws zipping through the streets—and the clamor of a town in constant motion. Ironically, I found more peace and quiet when I visited my mother in Guatemala City, where the chaotic energy seemed more contained.

The influx of tourism had dramatically altered the town's character. Foreigners and locals crowded into the hotels, restaurants, and bars, making it feel more like a tourist hotspot than a quaint lakeside town. On weekends, the once quiet nights were overtaken by blaring music from bars and clubs, shattering any hope of the peaceful retreat I had once envisioned. Mornings weren't much better—bombas from the Catholic church, firecrackers, and booming evangelical sermons echoed through the air, as if the town was caught in a battle of religious noise between Catholics and Evangelicals. The spiritual serenity I had once associated with the lake was completely drowned out.

As I settled into life in Pana, I began to see the darker side of its transformation. The nightlife, which in the past might have been filled with laid-back gatherings of like-minded souls, had taken a sharp turn. Strip clubs had sprung up, and what was once a place of peace and love had become more about sex, drugs, and rock and roll. By day, Pana was a chaotic metropolis, but by night, it morphed into a seedier version of Las Vegas.

The population of Panajachel, or Pana as it's affectionately called, is a diverse mix of ladinos—people of both indigenous and European heritage—and the Kachiquel-Maya, the indigenous group native to this region of Guatemala. Interwoven with this rich cultural tapestry is a community of expatriates, known locally as "gringos." While "gringo" once specifically referred to Americans, it has since broadened to encompass all foreigners who have settled around the lake, regardless of nationality.

Many of these expats, now well into their 70s, seem caught in a time warp, living out their later years in a bubble of nostalgia. They cling to the relics of their youth, still immersed in the counterculture habits of pot-smoking, drinking, and listening to classic rock—an echo of the free-spirited lifestyle that first drew them to Pana decades ago. It's as if time stopped for them somewhere in the haze of the '60s and '70s, and they continue to replay those years like an old record, scratched but familiar. Their routines, though comforting to them, create a peculiar atmosphere that feels oddly disconnected from the present.

While the world around them has moved on, reshaping Panajachel into a busy hub of tourism and commerce, these aging expats remain tethered to the past. The once revolutionary ideals they carried with them now seem frozen in time, as if they're living in a permanent state of youthful rebellion, despite the creases of age and the growing fragility of their bodies. For many of them, Pana offers a refuge from the complexities of modern life, a place where they can preserve the carefree essence of their younger selves.

And yet, in the midst of this nostalgia, the reality of Pana today—a place that has rapidly modernized—seems to clash with their dream of eternal "peace and love." The town's character has shifted, its cultural and economic landscape evolving, while they remain tethered to an era that no longer exists. Their presence is a poignant reminder of how dreams and memories can sometimes outlast the places that inspired them. Much like what I was experiencing.

However, as I had hoped, I found a position with Mayan Families shortly after my arrival. They had recently launched a new Medical Services department, and I was hired as the coordinator. The role was incredibly fulfilling. My main responsibility was to connect indigenous families in need with generous donors abroad, most of whom were American.

These donors, referred to as "padrinos," would send a monthly stipend, primarily to support the education of children within these families.

In my position, I extended the role of these padrinos by encouraging them to also step in during medical emergencies or when urgent needs arose in the families they were already sponsoring. It became a way to offer more holistic assistance to these communities, addressing both educational and medical vulnerabilities.

One of the most impactful aspects of my job was coordinating week-long dental care clinics, staffed by foreign volunteer dentists, much like Doctors Without Borders.

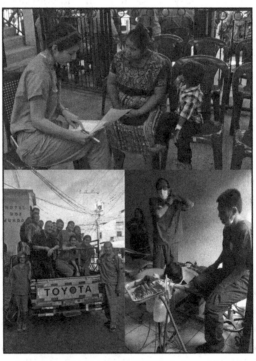

*"Dental Care week at Mayan Families,
Panajachel, Solola, Guatemala"*

I would also travel to remote villages to lead educational efforts aimed at improving health awareness, especially among the women who were responsible for their families' well-being. Surprisingly, one of the most pervasive health issues in these areas was diabetes. This was a staggering irony, considering that these families were growing some of the best fruits and vegetables in the region. But instead of consuming their harvest, these crops were sold for income, leaving the families to rely on cheap, unhealthy alternatives.

Even more shocking was the widespread consumption of soda as a replacement for water. Due to the lack of access to clean, potable water, sugary sodas had become a staple in many households, even for babies whose bottles were often filled with Coca-Cola instead of formula or milk. The consequences were dire, and witnessing this first-hand was eye-opening.

While the work was immensely rewarding, the financial aspect was another story. My position came with a volunteer stipend of only $500 a month, and living in Panajachel—now far more "cosmopolitan" and expensive than I remembered— was barely sustainable on such a modest income. The transformation of the town into a commercial hub had driven up the cost of living, making it difficult to stretch my small stipend far enough to cover basic expenses.

Fortunately, the TEFL certification I had earned as a backup plan turned out to be a lifeline. In August 2017, I secured a teaching position at The Robert Muller Life School of Panajachel, a bilingual institution where I became the 3rd grade teacher. This new role provided a steady income, which greatly alleviated the financial strain I had been under while working for Mayan Families. Sadly, the demands of teaching meant I had to step away from my position with Mayan Families, leaving behind the fulfilling work I had been doing in the Medical Services department.

As I transitioned into my new role as a teacher, I

found myself becoming more deeply immersed in the local community. Teaching offered me a new way to connect with both the children and their families, and it gave me a platform to continue making a meaningful impact. Although the work was different from my humanitarian efforts, it allowed me to foster a sense of purpose and stability.

Despite the many challenges—adapting to a new job, and navigating life in a town that had changed so drastically—I began to feel that I was finally carving out a place for myself. This new chapter was far from easy, but it was one where I could merge my passion for education with the deeper mission of serving the community.

"School picture of my 3rd Grade class from the Robert Muller Life School taken at the shores of Lake Atitlan, Panajachel, Solola, Guatemala"

When I joined the Robert Muller LIFE School in 2017, I became part of an institution that had long been a cornerstone of the Panajachel community. Established in 1988, the school was approaching its 30th anniversary the following year. It held a unique status, officially designated by the Guatemalan Ministry of Education as an "experimental" school—a label meant to distinguish it from more traditional educational institutions. The school had been founded by a group of expatriates with connections to the United Nations, and they had managed to persuade Robert Muller, then the Assistant Secretary-General of the UN, to visit, which led to the school being named in his honor.

While the school had once enjoyed theoretical support from the United Nations, that connection had long faded. Now, it functions as a bilingual school, its faculty largely made up of foreigners who sign a two year teaching agreement, while the local indigenous and Ladino staff work behind the scenes to keep the institution running. What might have once been a community-driven school with the student population being equally composed of both children of foreigners settled in the area and local indigenous children, had turned into an environment where entitlement and status overshadowed education. The parents seemed to view the teachers not as educators but as service providers tasked with catering to their expectations.

My teaching philosophy of nurturing responsibility and accountability clashed with the expectations of the parents of my students, who saw LIFE School as a status symbol for the wealthy Kachiquel-Maya elite of the area.

The hostility I faced from these parents was overwhelming. They resisted my efforts to instill discipline and accountability, and it became clear that they saw me as an obstacle to the pampered lives they envisioned for their children. My teaching philosophy combined with another issue, which was the true undercurrent for their dislike and distrust in me, was the fact that these parents saw me as a Guatemalan from the City, from the upper middle and "ruling" class of the nation.

To truly understand the social and economic complexities of Guatemala, it's crucial to delve into its history. As many of us learned in school, the Spanish conquest of the Americas that followed Columbus's infamous "discovery," led to the colonization by Spain of nearly all of Latin America, from the southern United States to Chile. The only significant exception was Brazil, which fell under Portuguese control.

Guatemala was once the heart of the Maya civilization, a highly sophisticated society that thrived long before the Spanish arrived. However, like so many indigenous cultures, the Maya were violently displaced, their land taken, and their way of life shattered. Labeled as "savages" by the European colonizers, they lost not only their ancestral territories—land they never saw as private property—but also their customs, religions, and languages. While Spanish became the official language, many Maya still speak their native tongues within their communities, maintaining fragments of their heritage amidst the enduring legacy of conquest.

The system of governance imposed by the Spanish was built on exploitation and brutal domination. The European settlers quickly became the landowners and wealthy elite, while the indigenous population was relegated to a life of poverty and labor. Education was deliberately withheld from the indigenous peoples, as keeping them uneducated and unaware of their rights was essential to maintaining control. The ruling class had no interest in empowering the majority to challenge the oppressive system.

The word *chapín* holds deep historical and cultural connotations in Guatemala, symbolizing much more than its surface meaning. Though commonly understood as a colloquial term to refer to all Guatemalans, its roots and implications run far deeper, especially in the context of the country's history. The term originates from a type of cork-soled overshoe from Spain, later used to describe fashionable shoes worn by nobles in the 15th century, the time of the Conquest. These shoes, with their high platforms and lined interiors, designed to keep the feet clean of mud, were uncomfortable but signified status, making a distinct "chap chap" sound with each step. Over time, *chapín* evolved to represent more than footwear—it came to embody notions of privilege, class, and power because they were only worn by the ruling class.

Guatemala's lengthy and brutal civil war, which lasted more than three decades, further embedded the social and ethnic divisions that had long shaped the country. The Maya, particularly those in the highlands near Lake Atitlán, suffered the most during this conflict, seeing the war as not just a political struggle but a battle against the *ladino* elite—descendants of Spanish colonizers who maintained their dominance over wealth and power. The term *chapín* began to take on a more pointed meaning, often referring to these wealthy, powerful families concentrated in Guatemala City. To the indigenous population particularly in the highlands, *chapines* were not just Guatemalans—they were the ruling class, a symbol of oppression and entrenched inequality.

Even today, the trauma of the civil war lingers, influencing the social dynamics and interactions across the country. As I experienced first hand. They saw me as a Chapina, despite the fact that I had lived most of my life in the United States, and even becoming an American citizen in 2014, I was still viewed through the lens of Guatemala's social hierarchy. In the eyes of many locals, I was a *Chapina*—an outsider, a member of the oppressive elite, regardless of my true intentions or background.

The hostility reached its peak when the parents of my third-grade students, united in their grievances, demanded a hearing. They wanted to confront me, armed with a list of absurd accusations, including one claim that I had physically kicked a student out of my classroom. The school administration, led by an American director and a curriculum coordinator also an American—neither of whom spoke Spanish fluently—quickly capitulated to the demands. To make matters worse, the president of the school board, a Colombian father of one of my students who clearly disliked me, was supposed to be my advocate but remained silent during the entire ordeal.

For two excruciating hours, I endured a barrage of baseless allegations, sitting on a stool while the angry parents surrounded me, accusing me of everything from being cruel to their children to deliberately sabotaging their learning. Any rational person might have walked out, but I stayed, for reasons I still can't fully explain. And somehow, despite this humiliating episode, I was asked to become the school's next director for the 2018-2019 academic year. How did that even happen? How did I let myself walk into such a disaster?

The previous director, the curriculum coordinator, and most of the American faculty were all leaving after fulfilling their two-year volunteer stints, leaving the newly arrived me—someone with experience in both American and Guatemalan cultures—as the logical candidate. I refused at least eight times, but slowly, my ego was stroked. I began to believe that I could bridge the gap between these two worlds, that I could somehow make a difference. Before I knew it, I had agreed, walking headfirst into what would become a year of immense frustration and emotional turmoil.

The challenges were insurmountable from the start. My indigenous Guatemalan staff and the new American faculty did not support me, and the school's board of directors—composed of the same parents who had once wanted me removed—were now my supposed bosses. It was doomed from the outset. The weight of unrealistic expectations, lack of backing, and underlying hostility made the year unbearable. I entered the position with good intentions, but I had vastly underestimated the depth of the resentment and the complexities of the environment I was stepping into.

To make matters worse, the LIFE School Foundation, initially created by former American directors, was falling apart. I had hoped to revive it and create a sustainable funding model, tapping into larger financial resources so that the school wouldn't have to rely solely on tuition. But instead, I found myself surrounded by individuals with ulterior motives, eager to exploit the foundation's 501(c)(3) tax-exempt status for their own gain. Rather than engage in a losing battle, the remaining American director decided to shut the foundation down, dividing the remaining scholarship funds among the neediest students before disappearing entirely. With the foundation gone, any hope of financial stability evaporated as well.

I had fled Chicago in a state of panic, overwhelmed by the growing fear that I could no longer afford to support myself in such an expensive city. My escape to Panajachel had been driven by the idea of living in what I thought was my "dream place." But I had rushed into it, forcing things to happen too quickly. Instead of allowing time to guide me, I pushed and pulled in every direction. And, as expected, when you push and pull too hard, things inevitably unravel—and unravel they did.

Once again, I found myself panicking. This time, I fled to Guatemala City, back to my mother's place. An enormous blow to my pride. Circumstances left me with no other choice.

Under the cover of night, I left Panajachel. My resignation from the position of school director came swiftly once I reached the city. As I sat in my mother's apartment, feelings of shame, fear, and anger swirled through my mind. Leaving Panajachel felt like the ultimate failure. I couldn't escape the sense that I had lost everything. My self-esteem, always fragile, was now completely shattered.

At that moment, I realized just how much my sense of self-worth had become dangerously dependent on external markers of success—achievements, material things, and validation from others. Without those, I felt as though I had nothing. Not even a place to call my own. I found myself trapped in a relentless cycle of self-judgment, constantly asking: How did I end up here? And worst of all, what now?

Once I settled into an empty room at mom's, the pressing question became: how would I make a living? What did I have to offer? The one thing that had always been reliable was my knowledge of the English language. So, I began searching for opportunities to teach English again, but there was one thing I knew for certain—I wasn't going back to teach at any other school ever again. That was a lesson I had already learned the hard way.

Desperate for work, I turned to the classified section of the local newspaper, *Prensa Libre.* Yes, I know—who reads newspapers anymore in this digital age? But they still exist, and my mom, true to form, is a loyal subscriber. That's where I found a job listing that caught my eye, and soon enough, I found myself hired as an English teacher with a language institute by the name of Berlitz. With over 150 years of global experience in language education, teaching professional adults who wanted to expand their English skills to advance in their careers, Berlitz seemed like a solid fit. At least I had a job!

But the reality was humbling. At 61 years old, I was filling out a long application to prove my proficiency in English, followed by a two-week intensive training program. I even had a supervisor—a young woman in her twenties. It felt degrading at times, but I needed the work. Despite the awkwardness, I was grateful to have the job, even if I was the oldest member of the team at the Guatemala City office.

However, the pay was far from sufficient. As many teachers know, the profession rarely pays enough, especially in Guatemala City. I needed something more substantial. That's when a new idea began to take shape. Inspired by the many successful entrepreneurs I had met in Guatemala, I decided to follow suit, take a leap of faith and open my own business.

I launched *STELLAR*, a tutoring service specializing in higher education preparation, with a focus on SAT and TOEFL exam prep. There was a growing demand for these services, especially among upper-class families who wanted to send their children to study in the United States. This was a field I knew well, and for the first time in a while, I felt a sense of confidence about my prospects.

I found a tiny office, just two blocks from Berlitz's main office in Zone 10—Guatemala City's bustling business district. The space was barely large enough to hold a desk and two chairs, but it was a start. Traffic in Zone 10 was notoriously heavy, so although I thought about walking to my tiny office like I had in Chicago or Panajachel, I was warned that it wasn't safe—walking in that area could easily make me a target for robbery. Nevertheless, I secured a six-month lease, giving myself just enough time to see if this venture would take off. It was a gamble, but it felt like the right move—a chance to reclaim some sense of control and chart a new course.

Then February 2020 arrived, and just as my six month lease was about to expire, the world was abruptly thrown into chaos—COVID-19 struck, and everything came to a grinding halt. It felt as if a new chapter was beginning, one that would overshadow all that had come before. While I won't delve into the global ramifications of the pandemic, it's enough to say that COVID-19 impacted everyone, and its effects continue to reverberate.

CHAPTER 17

"Keep reminding yourself of the way things are connected, of their relatedness. All things are implicated in one another and in sympathy with each other. This event is the consequence of some other one. Things push and pull on each other, and breathe together, and are one."

- Marcus Aurelius, Meditations

Fortunately, none of my immediate family members succumbed to the virus, and for that, I remain profoundly grateful. During the lockdown, my mom and I found ourselves cohabitating, which came with its own set of challenges, but at least we were not battling the loneliness that many faced. Berlitz quickly transitioned to an online format, utilizing Zoom, just like much of the world. Although teaching through a screen felt different, the technology allowed us to adapt. This transition kept us engaged and, more importantly, employed.

I also shifted *STELLAR* to an online format, but I lost my SAT and TOEFL clients as travel came to a standstill. When universities eventually reopened—albeit virtually— many eliminated SAT requirements in a desperate bid to attract students. As a result, that segment of my business evaporated. Yet, despite these setbacks, I managed to persevere. The trials brought on by the pandemic cultivated a newfound resilience within me.

So, amid both old and new challenges, I pressed on.

On July 5, 2020, I celebrated my 62nd birthday, and for the first time in my life, I genuinely looked forward to getting older. Why? Because reaching this milestone meant I could finally apply for early retirement. I wasted no time and submitted my application the very next month. On September 3, 2020, I received my first Social Security deposit, a moment that filled me with relief. After so long, I could finally take a deep breath. This financial security opened up the possibility of renting my own place.

Once again, I turned to the reliable classifieds in *Prensa Libre*. The very first apartment I circled on the newspaper felt like a perfect fit. It had everything I wanted: cozy, affordable, and centrally located. After making an appointment to see it, I walked through the door, and that single visit was all it took to confirm my decision. On September 19, 2020, I moved into Los Rincones, a charming one-bedroom apartment just a few blocks from my mom's place in a residential neighborhood. It was a fresh start.

That move was supposed to be a new chapter in my life, filled with independence and hope. As I unpacked in my Los Rincones apartment, I felt a brief moment of peace. But deep down, a challenge was looming—one that I could feel creeping closer, but I couldn't yet define. It felt like life was once again gearing up to test me, as it had so many times before.

By that point, I had already survived a lifetime of hardships—facing the fear of losing love, the uncertainty of work, and the gradual erosion of my self-worth. Every chapter of my life had been marked by trials that wore away my confidence, and the pandemic combined now with the AML diagnosis only magnified these struggles.

Yet, as daunting as it all felt, I knew I had no choice but to keep moving forward. I had been tested before and survived. This diagnosis, while terrifying, was just the next hurdle. With the weight of my past pressing down on me and the future shrouded in fear, I made a decision. I would face this new challenge not with despair, but with the hard-won resilience I had gained through a lifetime of overcoming adversity. The path ahead would be grueling, but I was determined to meet it head-on, with the strength I had earned.

PART 3

CHAPTER 18

*"It is through gratitude for the present moment
that the spiritual dimension of life opens up."*

- Eckhart Tolle

A Soul's Journey

Every human being is inherently unique. There is no such thing as a "generic" person, as each individual's uniqueness is shaped by the specific circumstances of their life—through their lineage, time, and space on Earth. It is through this lineage that I chose to return to human form, to witness and navigate the many challenges facing our planet and species at the cusp of a new millennium and a new era. The decision to incarnate was a courageous one, as there are no guarantees that you will remember your purpose, or find the other souls who agreed to join you on this journey.

I chose the year 1958, and the city of Guatemala as the starting point for this incarnation. I selected a Mediterranean ethnicity, choosing to be born as a fourth-generation Latin American heterosexual woman. My life would unfold in a relatively privileged socio-economic condition, where both the advantages and the limitations would equip me for the work I needed to do, and for the lessons my soul was still seeking.

That's why I chose to be part of a devoted Catholic family, full of contradictions to the very faith they claimed as their salvation. This would give me fertile ground to challenge, grow, and learn, guiding me toward my higher purpose.

Being raised in a Catholic household introduced me to an essential spiritual practice: the idea of Shared Sacredness. It was within this context of faith that I first encountered the concepts of devotion, sacrifice, and divine connection—concepts that would later become significant in my own spiritual evolution.

I chose Miguel Ángel Martini Padilla to be my father, a man who embodied the very masculine codes of his time. His life was defined by power, prestige, rank, and reputation, as well as upward mobility, honor, and the societal status that came with having a loyal, loving, and devoted wife. My mother, Myriam Stella Lainfiesta Castellanos, was that woman. She learned early in life the art of self-silencing and the weight of gendered social conditioning. These skills were crucial for her, as they allowed her to maintain "safe" relationships, especially in intimate settings, where submission was often seen as a virtue.

In choosing these two specific souls as my parents, I understood that I would be shaped by both the privileges and the burdens of their roles. My father's adherence to rigid masculine ideals and my mother's silent compliance would provide contrasting energies that I would need to navigate. From my father, I would witness the power dynamics of patriarchal authority. From my mother, I would see the toll that subservience to tradition can take on a woman's spirit. These dualities have been essential lessons for my soul's growth.

By coming into a life so deeply steeped in the rituals of faith, duty, and tradition, I knew I would be confronted with challenges that would test my sense of identity, purpose, and spiritual beliefs. I accepted this challenge willingly, for it was within this complex web of contradictions that my soul sought its evolution, expanding through experience and reflection.

I sought both the love and care that would be bestowed upon me, as well as the inevitable hurts that would be inflicted along the way. Each of these experiences have been vital in preparing me for the soul expansion work I have come here to do. They have shaped me, challenged me, and ultimately pushed me toward a deeper understanding of my purpose.

I also chose to be the eldest of my siblings. Being the firstborn in the Martini family played a crucial role in my formation. It established a sense of responsibility, leadership, and expectation that have guided my development.

"Mom for her 75th birthday with all her kids in tow in birth order: me, my brother Miguel, sister Ginna and little sister Myriam"

I was born without any physical disabilities, gifted with a strong mental constitution and an insatiable thirst for knowledge. Coupled with a highly sensitive spiritual awareness.

My purpose has been to grow in compassion and love—for everyone, for everything, in every place—and most importantly, toward myself. My journey would unfold at a time when humanity itself is undergoing its own profound transformation, and my soul's work is intrinsically linked to this collective shift. As I matured into adulthood and faced the challenges life presented—challenges that were not arbitrary but designed for my growth—I came to fully understand that Life was not something that happened *to* me; it was something happening *for* me.

Through these trials, I became increasingly aware of my true role: to be one of many sparks of light assisting in the galactic transition of humanity. I realized I was participating in the awakening of the New Earth, contributing to the elevation of human consciousness on a collective level. Just as the individual microcosm reflects the broader macrocosm, the personal journey mirrors the cosmic one. When we truly listen and open ourselves to the flow of the One Life Force, we begin to see that we are all active participants in this unfolding evolution.

In 1958, the world was still grappling with the aftermath of World War II. Though the war had ended, the pervasive fear remained, particularly with the looming threat of communism, which cast a long shadow over global politics, especially in the United States. My generation, the Baby Boomers, had witnessed unprecedented economic growth and newfound freedoms. But with those gains came an intense desire to protect what had been earned, especially against the perceived communist threat. The anxiety was heightened when the U.S. lost its Cuban stronghold to Fidel Castro's revolutionary movement, amplifying fears that communism would spread further into the Americas.

The horrors of Hiroshima and Nagasaki were still fresh in the global consciousness, vivid reminders of the devastating power of nuclear weapons. As the nuclear arms race between the United States and Russia intensified, the world teetered on the edge of uncertainty. The prospect of a Third World War, where two superpowers might press a button and unleash nuclear destruction, was a chilling reality no one wanted to confront.

Central America found itself thrust into this volatile landscape. Strategically positioned near the U.S., it became a region of critical importance in America's mission to secure its borders and prevent the spread of communism. The U.S., ever focused on its own interests, invested heavily in keeping its "backyard" safe, but paid little attention to the deep-rooted social and economic strife that had plagued the region since the Spanish conquest centuries earlier.

In Guatemala, the stark division between the Indigenous populations and the ruling Ladino class was more pronounced than ever. Centuries of oppression, inequality, and poverty festered into a growing resentment. And, with U.S. backing, the tension was armed and dangerous. Weapons flowed in, and specialized training was provided, further deepening the conflict. CIA operatives had settled in Guatemala, training select military factions to suppress the communist guerillas fighting their own brutal, dirty war.

I was not merely a distant observer of this conflict—I lived within it. As a young child, my life unfolded across the United States, Canada, and Guatemala, placing me at the crossroads of these two clashing worlds. I would bear witness to the casualties of this ideological battle, torn between the influence of the U.S. and the strife endured by my homeland. These early experiences of living between such contrasting cultures shaped my understanding of the world and set the foundation for the awareness I would carry into adulthood.

Every experience I've lived throughout my life has been a part of a vast, continuous classroom—one that has exposed me to the inhumanities, injustices, and prejudices that have shaped and strengthened my spirit. These challenges were not without purpose. They were necessary lessons, preparing me to channel the opposite forces of light, compassion, and open-mindedness in service to humanity during these critical times.

As Martin Luther King Jr. once said, "Peace is not merely a distant goal that we seek, but a means by which we arrive at that goal." His words resonate deeply with me, especially as I reflect on the turbulent times we are living in today—both in the United States and around the world. Democracy, once a hopeful beacon, seems to be hanging by a thread, while unimaginable devastation unfolds in places like Gaza. These events weigh heavily on my heart, and the urgency for justice feels more pressing than ever.

Justice has always been a guiding principle in my life, something deeply ingrained within me. It is impossible for me to disengage from the events that shape our world and the future we are building. Although I may not have the power to enact large-scale change, I am aware that even on a personal level, I can be one of those "sparks" of light—a witness, a voice, offering unwavering support and spreading compassion. It is easy to underestimate the power of our thoughts and intentions, but they are fundamental in shaping the collective consciousness. Each of us has a role to play in this global awakening.

We are living in an era where humanity is more interconnected than ever before. The Covid-19 pandemic underscored this truth, as the virus spread across borders and reminded us of our shared vulnerability. Technology, too, has brought us closer, placing the power of information at our fingertips. We now bear witness to the transgressions against our planet and our fellow humans with greater immediacy, the brutality of these injustices impossible to ignore.

In such times, it is more important than ever to cultivate a discerning mind, to stay grounded in truth rather than allowing ourselves to be fed a toxic diet of misinformation rooted in hate, greed, and the last desperate attempts of the imperial forces that have long ruled our world. The tides are shifting, and now is the moment for us to stand firm in the light, guided by a vision of peace, justice, and compassion that will carry us into a new era.

Indeed, we are witnessing the dawn of a New Era—the Age of Aquarius—where a profound shift in consciousness is unfolding. There is a long-awaited return to balance as the Divine Feminine energy rises once more, emerging from the ashes where it had been buried for centuries by the forces of patriarchy. This energetic resurgence signals the end of an era defined by imbalance, and it is precisely why we are experiencing such turbulence in the world today.

These are the final, desperate throes of a fading energy, an old paradigm that knows its time is ending. It will not pass quietly. Instead, it lashes out, grasping at power and control, kicking and screaming like a child being grounded, resisting the inevitable change. The chaos we see around us is not a sign of failure, but of transition—an unraveling of the old to make space for the new.

It is in this precise moment that my soul was always meant to be. Every experience, every challenge, every joy and sorrow in my life has been in preparation for this. The journey I have walked, marked by the complexities and lessons of human existence, has been necessary to shape me into who I am today. It has brought me to this point of awareness, to this understanding that the turbulence we face is not the end but the beginning of something greater—a reawakening of balance, love, and unity on a global scale. This is why my soul elected to incarnate in this lifetime, to witness and contribute to this monumental shift in human consciousness.

But before I could move forward, fate had one more test in store for me—a relapse that affected me physically, mentally, and emotionally. It was as if my Ultimate Teacher, ever patient, was reinforcing the lessons I had yet to fully learn. Like any diligent instructor, there needed to be an evaluation, a reckoning, to measure how far I had come and what I still needed to confront. This setback, though painful, was a reminder that growth is rarely linear, and sometimes, the hardest challenges are the ones that push us closest to the Truth.

CHAPTER 19

"Forgiveness is not a favor we offer to those who wronged us. It is a gift we give to ourselves, for it frees us from the burden of bitterness."

- Br. David Steindl-Rast

By the end of 2022 and feeling empowered after reaching remission so quickly, I was eager to spend the holidays with my children. I had high hopes for this reunion, imagining it as a time of joy, healing, and connection. But instead, those expectations crumbled. An unexpected breakup cast a shadow over everything, turning what should have been a loving family gathering into an emotionally devastating experience. I returned to Guatemala on January 31, 2023, not with the sense of fulfillment I had anticipated, but with a heart broken and a spirit weighed down by the emotional wreckage.

Despite everything I had learned from my encounter with leukemia, all the personal growth and introspection I thought I had achieved, it felt like those lessons vanished. As I settled back into my apartment in Los Rincones, the dark emotions crept in. Self-doubt, anger, and overwhelming sadness began to suffocate me. I felt disconnected from the person I had hoped to become, like all the progress I had made was slipping through my fingers. The emotional spiral was relentless, making me question my worth, my strength, and my ability to move forward.

By February, it was time for my six-month check-up. Despite my emotional state, I wasn't physically concerned—I felt fine, and believed I was still in remission. But my oncologist insisted on a full range of tests—blood work, ultrasounds, a mammogram. It seemed unnecessary, but for peace of mind, I agreed. When the lab results came back, disbelief washed over me. I had grown accustomed to reading my own reports, and the numbers were glaringly wrong. Everything was out of balance, a far cry from the clean results I had seen just months before.

My oncologist, equally stunned, ordered another bone marrow extraction. The confirmation hit like a blow: I had relapsed. More chemotherapy was required—multiple rounds, just like the first time. My initial reaction was rejection. I couldn't bear the thought of going through it all over again. The memories of the physical pain, the emotional exhaustion, and the isolation came rushing back. But after discussions with my brother and my doctor, both of whom had faith in the treatment plan, I reluctantly agreed to proceed.

This time, my veins—already ravaged by the previous chemotherapy—were no longer reliable, so a port was installed in my chest. It was supposed to be a simple, "minor" surgery, but it turned out to be anything but. The anesthesia hit me harder than expected, and I was left bedridden for over a week. Alone in my apartment, the physical discomfort was compounded by the emotional strain. I was filled with doubt, constantly asking myself, *Why am I doing this again? Is this truly the only path forward? Do I even have the strength to do this again?*

The relapse felt like a betrayal, not just by my body, but by the universe itself. I had worked so hard, and now, it felt like everything was unraveling. The weight of both physical and emotional exhaustion was overwhelming, leaving me questioning everything.

As I prepared to face another round of treatments following my relapse, my therapist, who had been pivotal in my initial recovery, strongly urged me to continue therapy. She believed it would help me mentally and emotionally to process the difficult medical journey ahead. Friends also rallied around me, offering support in unexpected ways. A couple of them, deeply immersed in "A Course in Miracles," invited me to a seminar led by the renowned Spanish professor, José Luis Molina. Although it was aimed at clinical therapists, they insisted I join, believing it could offer me a new perspective in healing.

Curiosity and an open heart led me to accept their offer. From the moment I walked into the seminar, I felt an undeniable sense of reassurance. Greeted by a towering statue of Archangel Michael, I couldn't help but feel that I was exactly where I needed to be. This particular session was centered around forgiveness—more specifically, "expiation," a concept I hadn't fully explored before. I had always understood forgiveness as a necessity, not for the benefit of the person who wronged me, but for myself. Forgiving didn't mean condoning the act, but it released me from carrying the burden of resentment.

Expiation, however, took this a step further. As José Luis explained, it wasn't just about letting go; it was about actively removing the emotional "debris" that weighed on the soul, much like throwing away trash with force and purpose. It was about healing from a place of strength, not weakness or victimhood. Atonement, he said, was essential—it was about clearing the obstacles that stood between us and the divine.

The session took an unexpected turn when José Luis asked me, "Why are you here?" I started to explain my recent relapse of Acute Myeloid Leukemia. He paused and, with a slight smile, began to search for more information about the condition on his phone. Before he could finish, a man in the audience, a doctor named Miguel, stood up. He offered a clear, clinical explanation of AML, describing how my white blood cells were multiplying rapidly but failing to mature. Their inability to fully develop left my immune system vulnerable, and the rapid accumulation of immature cells was what made the disease so dangerous. Miguel's calm, authoritative tone reminded me of Archangel Michael's protective presence.

With the explanation behind us, José Luis steered the session back to me. He asked me to imagine myself as a young child, inviting him to my home after school. "Where is your mother?" he asked gently. I searched my memories but found nothing. All I could think about was wanting to be at my grandparents' house instead. The realization hit me like a wave—I had always felt most safe and loved with my grandmother, not my mother, whom I truly adore. That revelation opened a floodgate of memories and emotions, feelings I had buried deep for so long.

As we dug deeper, I began to realize that my relationship with my mother had been fraught with feelings of abandonment and neglect. I hadn't quite understood it before, but now it was clear. My father's career and needs always came first, and my mother, perhaps out of her own sense of duty or love, followed him. We, my brother and I, were left behind, secondary characters in the drama that was my father's life.

These realizations hit me profoundly. I had always carried feelings of unworthiness, insecurity, and neglect, but until that moment, I hadn't fully understood their origins. My mother had never truly stood up for us, never prioritized us over my father. To clarify, when I say "us," I mean my brother and me; my younger sisters came along much later, a decade apart from us. During our childhood, my mother had chosen him repeatedly, and that choice left a lasting imprint on my sense of self-worth.

As José Luis guided me through this process, I began to see how this deeply rooted pain had affected my entire life. My relationships, my self-esteem, and even my ability to forgive myself were all tainted by this childhood wound. It became clear that forgiveness, in this case, wasn't just about my mother or even my father—it was about "expiation" of the feelings of abandonment, hurt, and rejection I had carried for so long. It was about releasing myself from the grip of the past so that I could heal, not just physically from leukemia, but emotionally and spiritually from the pain that unconsciously had shaped me.

At that moment, I understood that the true confrontation wasn't just with the cancer in my body—it was with the unresolved pain in my heart. And only through forgiveness and expiation could I hope to fully heal.

The explanation Miguel gave that day about Acute Myeloid Leukemia resonated deeply. As he spoke about how the bone marrow frantically produces white blood cells that never fully mature, leaving the body defenseless, I began to see a striking parallel to my own life. From a very young age, I had internalized the belief that I was on my own—that no one else was there to take care of me, so I had to do it myself. Just like those immature white blood cells, I was operating in survival mode, always busy, always producing, but never reaching the point where I could truly feel protected and safe. I was stuck in a cycle of incomplete growth, physically, mentally, emotionally and spiritually.

This limiting belief—the sense of being utterly alone— seeped into every corner of my life. At every stage, life seemed to conspire to reinforce it. By 17, I was already pregnant, following in my mother's footsteps, and soon found myself married to a man who embodied the same archetype that dominated the men in my family. He, like them, was cloaked in machismo and bravado, projecting authority while being incapable of truly caring for himself or his family without the constant nurturing of a wife. My grandfather had been this way, and so had my father—men who demanded control, their masculinity rigid and dominant on the surface, but beneath that tough exterior was emotional immaturity and dependency. Their bravado was a mask, concealing the truth that they relied on the "motherly" care of their wives to function, all the while expecting subservience in return.

Growing up in Guatemala during the '60s and '70s, I saw this dynamic play out not only in my own family but in the broader culture. In a country steeped in patriarchy, under the heavy influence of Catholicism, men were seen as the heads of the household, the providers, the decision-makers. Yet, ironically, they could barely take care of themselves. It was the women—meek, submissive, and often burdened with the weight of their husband's emotional and physical needs—who held the household together. These women were the caretakers, yet their roles were overshadowed by a societal structure that rendered them invisible, powerless. My mother had lived this reality, as had my grandmother before her.

In many ways, I had unconsciously followed that same path. I, too, married a man who couldn't fully stand on his own, who needed me to be the caretaker, the steady one. Like the immature white blood cells in my body, neither of us ever reached a point of true maturity or independence. We were locked in a dance of dependency, neither one able to break free from the roles that had been imposed on us by generations of patriarchal conditioning.

As I reflected on this, it became clear that my limiting belief of being alone had shaped every major decision I had made. I had taken on the role of caretaker because I didn't believe anyone else would care for me. I had settled into relationships where I was the nurturer because that was what I had been taught to expect. But in doing so, I had never allowed myself to fully grow, to truly mature into the person I was meant to be.

The parallel between my white blood cells and my own emotional state was undeniable. Both were frantically working, trying to fulfill a role they were never meant to carry alone. And in both cases, the result was the same—an inability to thrive, to fully realize their potential. Just as my white blood cells failed to protect me, my belief that I had to do everything on my own had failed to protect my heart, my spirit.

This realization was profound. For the first time, I understood that my journey with leukemia wasn't just about dealing with a physical disease. It was also about confronting the emotional wounds and limiting beliefs that had been festering inside me for decades. It was about recognizing that I wasn't truly alone, that I didn't have to carry the weight of the world by myself. And it was about allowing myself to finally grow—to mature in ways that I had been too afraid to before.

At that moment, I knew that my healing had to go beyond chemotherapy. It had to include healing the parts of me that had always believed I was destined to be alone, to be the caretaker, to never fully receive care myself. Only by confronting those beliefs could I hope to move forward, to allow my body and soul to fully recover. And perhaps, just like those white blood cells, I could finally grow into the strength I had always carried within me but had never fully realized.

This is where the true expiation began. As I came to terms with the harsh truths I had been subconsciously avoiding. Along with this, a profound understanding dawned on me of why my body had been ravaged by this disease. With that realization came a peace that only the Divine could provide. And, perhaps most importantly, through forgiveness.

I began to release all those limiting beliefs I had held about my mother. In doing so, I forgave her, and more critically, I forgave myself. Forgiveness, after all, is a gift we give to ourselves, a bridge that connects us to healing. I realized how I had carried the weight of resentment for years, unconsciously blaming her for the neglect I perceived in my childhood. But with this newfound clarity, I understood that her limitations were not a reflection of her love for me, nor of my worth. They were simply the manifestations of her own struggles, just as my own shortcomings had played out in my relationship with my daughter.

The estrangement between my daughter and me has been a source of deep pain, but now I could see it for what it truly is: not a failure of love, but perhaps a failure of availability. Just as I had sought comfort from my paternal grandmother rather than my mother, my daughter may have needed me in ways I wasn't fully present for. She knows I love her, just as I always knew my parents loved me. Yet, there was a disconnect—a gap between love and presence.

And as this understanding settled in, I felt a profound wave of relief wash over me, like a balm soothing old wounds. The act of forgiveness—both for my mother and for myself— lifted the burden I had been carrying for so long.

After the session, Jose Luis rose and handed me my "prescription," a simple yet powerful set of affirmations to guide me in the days and months to come:

- I have handed this over.
- God does not want me to suffer from this again.
- I am ready to receive the miracle that
this situation is offering me.

As I glanced around the room, I saw others in tears, touched by the healing they had witnessed through my experience. At that moment, I understood that healing is not a solitary journey. It radiates outward, touching others in ways we may never fully comprehend.

I have been the recipient of a miracle, not just in the physical sense, but in the deeper transformation of the heart. Through forgiveness—of my mother, of myself, and of my daughter—something sacred has been restored within me. I have found peace, and with it, a renewed capacity to love without barriers.

This is where things took a truly fascinating turn. After returning home from that deeply transformative experience, my mind was soon flooded with doubts. The biggest question gnawed at me: should I even proceed with chemotherapy? Hadn't I just experienced a full-blown miracle? If I had truly been blessed in such a profound way, was it not a sign that the disease had been healed? But then another fear crept in—was my skepticism about the miracle enough to undo the blessing I had received?

It wasn't just me who felt this uncertainty. Even my therapist, who had been with me throughout this journey, expressed similar concerns. She advised me to reach out to Miguel, the physician who had been present during my session, the one who had offered such a clear and thoughtful explanation about AML.

I contacted Miguel, and his response was nothing short of enlightening. He said, *"Don't worry about anything. You must follow the doctor's advice and treat your body with the means available in this world. Remember, Jesus teaches us that we cannot perform miracles while gripped by fear, as long as we remain in this dream called life. Nothing here is real—everything merely *seems* real. It seems like you have cancer. It seems like you have financial problems. But by understanding that everything only *seems* real, we strip away its power over us."*

His words continued. *"And remember the sacred word I mentioned: 'momentarily.' You must do everything momentarily. Take the chemo, the medicine, whatever is needed—for now. All of this is temporary until your belief in the miracle is total and complete. In the meantime, you act in the world, but you remind yourself that this is only momentary."*

At first, I struggled to grasp the full depth of his message. It was comforting, yes, but part of me hadn't fully internalized it. Yet, his words gave me the permission I sought to move forward with the treatment. I didn't have to choose between faith in the miracle and medical intervention—I could do both. The miracle was not invalidated by taking chemotherapy; the two could coexist. I began to understand that this physical healing journey was not separate from the spiritual one.

This revelation wasn't just about my body being healed. It was a realization that the miracle had already begun, not only in the physical realm but in the way I understood my existence. The miracle wasn't just the removal of illness; it was the shift in my perception of life, the transformation of my fear into faith, and my understanding of reality into something far more profound.

The miracle was unfolding within me, moment by moment. And as I embraced it, I saw that the doubts were simply part of the process, not a denial of the miracle but a necessary step toward fully receiving it.

CHAPTER 20

*"I think there is no suffering greater than what is
caused by the doubts of those who want to believe. I
know this torment so well. But I also know that God
will never let us down if we remain open to Him."*

– Mother Teresa

During that latest trip to South Bend, Indiana, I had also
longed to meet up with my dear friend Barbara. Our friendship,
which began when she was our immigration attorney, had
deepened over the years, evolving into something far more
profound. Barbara had been diagnosed with breast cancer
at least seven years prior. She endured a partial mastectomy,
followed by rounds of chemotherapy and radiation. While
she went into remission for a time, it didn't last. Her cancer
returned, and now it had spread to her lungs.

We stayed connected through phone calls and emails, but
I desperately wanted to spend real, face-to-face time with her.
That's the kind of friendship we had. However, when I arrived
in South Bend, I learned that her health had taken a sharp
decline. She had been hospitalized, struggling to breathe. I was
deeply disappointed, knowing that I wouldn't get the chance to
see her. It felt like a missed opportunity, and yet I held on to
the hope that we would have another moment together.

Our last exchange came through email on January 14th, 2023:

"Dear Blanqui,

I'm sorry I missed you. My cancer has metastasized and I spent Christmas and another week in the hospital with pneumonia. They have started infusions but had to cancel while I've been in the hospital. Please send me healing energy. I want to get better.

Love you, Barbara"

I responded with all the love and hope I could muster:

"My dear sweet sister, of course I will send you all my healing energy and will put you in my prayer circle of powerful, intentional women.

Know that love is the highest energy in the Universe and that you are always surrounded by it.

Sending you all the light and healing nurturing energy."

Barbara passed away on February 7th, 2023. I found out on February 10th, just days after discovering that I, too, had relapsed. It was as if the universe had conspired to deal me blow after blow.

During that same ill-fated trip to South Bend, I did manage to visit Dora, another friend and former colleague from my time at IUSB. Dora had been diagnosed with stage 4 uterine cancer around the same time I was undergoing my first chemotherapy treatment in 2021. Our mutual colleagues had reconnected us, thinking my optimism and positive outlook could inspire Dora, who wasn't taking her diagnosis as well. Dora had always viewed life through a lens of unfairness, seeing herself as a victim of circumstance, despite her immense talent. She was a gifted artist, her sculptures known worldwide, yet she seemed to embody the gloomy figure of Eeyore from *Winnie the Pooh*.

Initially, I had resisted reconnecting with her, daunted by her pessimism. But eventually, compassion overtook my reluctance. I reached out, offering her my most sincere advice about staying positive, especially when facing something as daunting as cancer. To me, a hopeful mindset was key to any effective treatment.

By the time we visited, Dora had shifted her outlook. She was navigating her treatments with more grace, even though they were harsh. She couldn't eat and was being fed through a tube, but her spirit was stronger. Her son Andreas, only 27, was her sole caretaker, having quit his job and moved back into her home to care for her full time. It was a burden he carried with incredible devotion. My heart ached for him, and yet I admired his resilience.

Then, in a cruel twist of fate, the roles reversed. By March 10th, 2023, Dora was the one offering me words of encouragement, as I prepared for another bone marrow biopsy to determine if I had relapsed. She reached out again on March 18th, the same day I experienced my miracle with Jose Luis Molina. As I faced a looming decision about hospitalization and starting another round of chemotherapy, I was still grappling with the loss of Barbara and the uncertainty of my own health.

On April 7th—Holy Friday—Dora sent me a message, wishing me a "Buona Pasqua" in her native Italian. She asked if I had decided on my treatment, and I explained that I had postponed it for two reasons: first, my doctor was scheduling around his Easter vacation, and second, I was in the process of moving to Lake Atitlán. I needed clarity and strength for the move, and I insisted that I, not the doctor, should choose when to begin treatment.

She replied with her usual grace, telling me about her upcoming CT scan and chemotherapy. "I hope you have ideas about some other treatment that isn't chemo," she wrote. I assured her I didn't, and signed off with my usual "take care, kisses and hugs."

On Easter Sunday, April 9th, I sent her a beautiful quote from Basil C. Hume: "*The great gift of Easter is hope.*"

I never received a reply.

The next day, April 10th, as Andreas was driving Dora to Northwestern Hospital for her treatment, they were involved in a tragic accident. Their car hit the back of a UPS semi-truck, crushing the passenger side and killing Dora instantly. Andreas, sitting in the driver's seat, was completely unharmed.

When I received the news, I felt numb. Then, a wave of searing anger hit me, directed squarely at God. What kind of God would allow something like this? I could accept that Dora's death may have brought her relief from her suffering, but did it have to happen in front of her son? Did it have to be so cruel, so sudden?

The grief I had already been carrying—from Barbara's passing, from my own relapse with cancer—suddenly felt insurmountable. I couldn't reconcile this tragedy in my mind, much less in my heart, which was already drowning in sorrow. How was I supposed to make sense of a world where love and loss were so intertwined, where grief was a constant companion on this fragile journey through life?

Apprehension weighed heavily on me as I faced the decision to begin infusions for the fifth time in just over two years. I was in no state—mentally, emotionally, or physically—to handle it. Doubts swirled in my mind like dark clouds, and with every passing moment, they only grew thicker. I couldn't shake the feeling that something was wrong, that I wasn't ready, and that my body wasn't prepared for the ordeal it would soon face.

What made matters worse was my oncologist's vague and often unclear communication. He was a busy man, an "exclusive" doctor at Hospital Centro Médico, where he managed at least two full floors of patients at any given time. This left him with little room for detailed explanations or reassurances. His hurried demeanor and constant juggling between patients left me feeling like just another number, not someone in need of care and clarity.

It didn't help that I had heard unsettling stories about some of his patients. A few had gone in for treatment, only to die shortly after, some never leaving the hospital, others given a clean bill of health only to succumb to a different, undiagnosed cancer. With each tale, my confidence in his abilities wavered. I was already grappling with my own fear, but these stories made it so much worse.

The truth was, I was terrified. Fear gripped me in a way it hadn't before. Fear of the unknown, of what my body would endure, of how much more I could take. I postponed the chemotherapy, telling my oncologist and my family that I needed to move to the house at Lake Atitlán and close up my apartment in the city first. This was true, but the reality was that I was desperately seeking any reason to delay. I wasn't ready to face it yet.

I had secured a house-sitting arrangement with an Englishman who owned a beautiful property, *The Four Pillars*, in San Pablo La Laguna, Atitlán. It was supposed to be a peaceful retreat, a place where I could convalesce. But beneath the surface, fear, loneliness, and anger were consuming me. These emotions coursed through me like a relentless tide, dragging me under. I knew I was not in a good place, mentally or emotionally, to begin such a delicate treatment.

Eventually, though, I dutifully complied. On April 25th, I was admitted to the hospital for yet another round of chemotherapy. But the anxiety that had been gnawing at me from the inside was immediately validated by the incompetence I encountered. On that very first day, the hospital failed to administer the chemotherapy because they hadn't ordered the medications. When the medicines did arrive, they were the wrong ones. It was a comedy of errors—except none of it was funny. I was so outraged by the ineptitude that they finally discounted that entire day of hospitalization.

But the incompetence didn't end there. The nurses—if they could even be called that—were woefully unskilled. They couldn't properly use the outdated vital signs machines, which were in disrepair. My oncologist greeted me with a casual, "Here we go again," as though this were just another day in the office. Worse still, he introduced a completely different chemotherapy regimen than the one I had previously responded well to. He had said before that I had reacted positively to the earlier treatment, but now he decided to switch to a more expensive and, ultimately, ineffective combination of drugs.

I was put on Idarubicin and Cytarabine—a regimen, he said, used specifically for relapsed acute myeloid leukemia. Idarubicin, like the Doxorubicin I had taken during my first treatment, is an anthracycline, a cytotoxic drug that works by poisoning cancer cells. But like any poison, it came with devastating side effects. My body, already weakened, did not respond well at all.

When I was discharged 5 days later, I clung to the hope that I could recover at Lake Atitlán. I left the hospital, believing I was in good condition, and planned to spend a few days with my mother before heading to the lake. But within those first days, my body began to fail me. It started with agonizing stomach cramps, which quickly spiraled into a severe intestinal infection. I was hit with uncontrollable diarrhea and a high fever. I could barely move, and my poor 83-year-old mother wasn't able nor equipped to take care of me.

In desperation, I reached out to my brother and sister-in-law for help. I arrived at my brother's apartment in a state of near-collapse, completely dehydrated and suffering from fainting spells. This wasn't what I had expected at all. I had endured side effects from chemotherapy before, but nothing like this. My red blood cell count and platelets plummeted, and I was soon in need of urgent blood transfusions and apheresis, a procedure I had never heard of.

Apheresis involves removing blood from a donor, separating it in a lab, and reintroducing plasma back into the patient's body to treat autoimmune conditions. Finding donors proved difficult. Many of my friends and family members were either too old or unable to donate, and the hospital didn't have the facilities to handle the procedure. They outsourced everything.

I was scheduled to return to the hospital for outpatient transfusions, but the port that had been surgically implanted in my chest couldn't be used, so they had to administer the transfusions intravenously. I called an anesthesiologist I trusted, unwilling to let anyone else attempt the procedure. After all the missteps at the hospital, I could trust no one. Even the elevators weren't working when I arrived. I had to climb two flights of stairs, weak and anemic, taking only a few steps at a time.

The transfusions, which were meant to save my life, took nearly ten hours, from 9am to 7pm, in a tiny room that felt more like a closet than a proper medical space. By the time I was discharged, I was a shell of myself, barely able to function.

Returning to my brother's apartment, I continued the aftercare, including painful injections of Filgrastim around my belly button to help stimulate white blood cell production. But despite the care and love I received from my family, I felt utterly alone. Weak, disoriented, and wracked with dizzy spells that triggered alarming arrhythmias, I was a prisoner of my own body.

All I could do was hold on, desperately clinging to the hope that I would live long enough to see my sons. Both Canche and Ricky were set to arrive at the lake on May 20th, and Danny on June 21st. That became my singular focus, the goal that kept me moving forward. I followed every instruction, underwent every test, and adhered strictly to the dietary plan. Outwardly, I was the model patient, doing everything right, but inside, I was broken.

I wept. I prayed. I begged God to give me the strength to make it through, to see my sons, and to return to the house at the lake, where I believed my heart truly belonged.

CHAPTER 21

"Words have power. Words can light fires in the minds of men. Words can wring tears from the hardest hearts."

- Elizabeth Lesser, "Cassandra Speaks"

On May 21st, 2023, Canche, Ricky and I were finally en route to Lake Atitlán, heading to The Four Pillars—a retreat I had been anticipating for weeks. I was thrilled to be there, yet beneath that excitement, I was concealing a far deeper struggle.

It was during this time that the idea of stopping chemotherapy began to take root. The thought had surfaced before, but I brushed it off, assuming it was a passing reaction to the side effects and the emotional weight of being hospitalized. But now, that whisper had grown louder, refusing to be ignored.

Eventually, I couldn't keep it to myself any longer. I confided in both Canche and Ricky, telling them I was seriously considering ending my chemotherapy. To my surprise, they took the news well. We talked through every aspect, especially the financial burden. They were concerned that money might be a factor in my decision, but I assured them it wasn't the main issue, though it did weigh on me. I knew how expensive the treatments were, even in Guatemala, but it was nowhere near what they would cost in the U.S. without insurance.

It was a heartfelt conversation, one filled with emotions

and tears, because discussing the possibility of stopping treatment meant confronting the harsh reality that it could reduce my chances of recovery. But there it was, laid bare: I was seriously considering walking away from chemotherapy.

After a month-long stay with me at The Four Pillars, Canche had to return to the U.S. We left Lake Atitlán a few days early to say goodbye to the rest of the family in the city. At my brother's insistence, I went for a follow-up blood test, which revealed alarming results: all my blood counts—red cells, hemoglobin, white cells, lymphocytes—were critically low.

That evening, before the family gathered for a farewell dinner for Canche, my brother pulled me aside. His voice was serious as he asked when I planned to resume chemo, urging me to contact my oncologist. I didn't tell him the whole truth— that I was seriously considering not continuing at all. Instead, I dodged the issue, saying I wanted to wait until after Danny's visit to decide. He wasn't happy with my answer, but he didn't push further, though I could see the worry in his eyes. He believed I needed to return to the hospital soon.

My oncologist had a similar reaction when he saw my lab results. His response was immediate: "If you feel very tired, you should get at least two more units of blood transfusions." That was always his go-to recommendation. He then asked, what I thought he should be the one to know: "When did we last administer chemo?" When I told him it had been over a month, he simply said, "Yes, you're overdue for your next round."

That conversation on June 9th, 2023, was the last exchange I had with him about chemotherapy. I hadn't made the final decision yet, but deep down, I knew that chapter, particularly under his care, was closing.

In today's healthcare system, patients are often treated as commodities, with the focus skewed heavily toward treating symptoms rather than preventing illness. This system, driven by protocols, statistics, and standardizations, can strip away the recognition of our human uniqueness and the intricate interconnections within the whole body. Physicians often enter the field with a profound desire to heal, but their training emphasizes the mechanical and chemical aspects of the human body, sidelining the subtleties that make each individual unique. Their work revolves around averages and outcomes, with little attention paid to the nuanced and holistic needs of the person before them.

As a result, what we have is not truly a healthcare system but an "illness care" system, addressing breakdowns only after they occur. Physicians in this model are akin to mechanics: highly skilled at diagnosing and repairing damage but rarely involved in maintaining the overall health and balance of the "vehicle"—in this case, the human body. Yet unlike machines, we are far more complex, extending beyond our bones and organs into a realm of subtle energy that modern medicine barely acknowledges. This energetic layer—the essence of our being—remains largely uncharted, though it profoundly influences our physical, mental, and emotional well-being.

My father was a brilliant physician, trained at some of the world's most prestigious institutions and celebrated for his surgical expertise. His walls were lined with diplomas and accolades, a testament to his dedication and skill. Patients trusted and adored him, and his ability to save lives in critical situations like appendicitis or trauma showcased the undeniable strengths of Western medicine. Yet even in his remarkable career, the subtle, energetic aspects of human health—the interplay of mind, body, and spirit—were not part of the equation.

Growing up in a household shaped by the values of modern medicine, I held deep respect for the scientific advancements that have extended and improved countless lives. The achievements of Western medicine are monumental, and the gratitude I feel for the doctors and technology that treated me is immeasurable. For a long time, I placed unwavering faith in the system, trusting that its methods would lead to healing and wholeness. And for a while, they did.

But eventually, that system fell short.

This realization led me to question whether true healing could come solely from conventional treatments or if a more holistic approach was needed—one that addresses the full spectrum of our humanity, including the delicate, often-ignored energy fields that underpin our physical existence. My journey has deepened my gratitude for the medical professionals who guided me and for my father's legacy, but it has also opened my eyes to the limitations of a system that views us primarily as a collection of symptoms and statistics.

Healing is far more than fixing what's broken; it's about understanding and nurturing the whole person. For me, embracing this truth has been both a challenge and a liberation—an invitation to explore dimensions of health that science has yet to fully comprehend.

As I grappled with my decision on whether or not to stop chemotherapy, I realized I was no longer blindly trusting in the system. I was questioning it. I was shifting my focus from the physical treatment of symptoms to the broader, deeper aspects of my well-being—the parts of me that Western medicine simply couldn't touch. It was time to step off that well-worn path and explore what it truly meant to heal, not just from illness in the body, but also in the mind, and spirit.

I saw The Four Pillars as a sanctuary for healing, a place where I could begin a holistic journey toward wholeness. Armed with the knowledge I had gathered from the worlds of metaphysics and the esoteric, which blend science and spirituality, I was ready to embrace a new approach to healing. One thing became abundantly clear to me along the way—the immense power of words. Words are more than just tools for communication; they carry energy, intention, and weight. They shape our reality, so we must wield them with care.

When I was first diagnosed, the language surrounding cancer was suffocating. The immediate reaction, from society and even from well-meaning loved ones, was to encourage me to "fight" the disease, to become a warrior, to go to war. But deep down, I recoiled at the idea of waging a battle against my own body. The language of war felt all wrong. Since the 1960s and 70s, it seemed that everything was framed as a war—war on drugs, war on poverty, war on cancer. War, war, war. But what has this mindset brought us, really? More pain, more suffering, more death. There are no true winners in a war, only endless cycles of destruction.

Take the "war on cancer" that was declared in 1971 by Richard Nixon, alongside the infamous war on drugs. Nixon signed the National Cancer Act, promising that increased research and new drug therapies would "eradicate" cancer. Fifty years later, despite all our technological advances, cancer still claims more than half a million lives each year. The war metaphor made cancer seem like an enemy to be vanquished, something to be killed. And while targeted therapies have made strides, the battle is far from over, and the victories are small compared to the massive losses.

Wars—whether they be political, social, or medical—are often driven by power and control, by domination. And in any war, someone or something is oppressed, defeated, or destroyed. This was not the energy I wanted to bring into my healing process. From the moment I was diagnosed, I consciously chose to reject the language of combat, of battling and conquering. Instead, I wanted to approach this experience with gentleness, acceptance, and understanding. But even as I chose kinder words, I failed to fully realize that I was still submitting myself to treatments rooted in the very idea of "killing" the cancer.

Dr. Gabor Maté, a physician who explores the mind-body connection in healing, aptly said, "*It may be that these material metaphors (war metaphors) are so appealing because their force matches our feelings of anger and despair; that does not, however, make them helpful."* His words resonated with me deeply. There's something seductive about the idea of fighting back when we feel powerless, but that doesn't mean it's the right approach.

With the relapse of AML, I came to understand this on a deeper level. Only focusing on chemotherapy does not always equal better results. Sometimes, it only compounds the suffering without delivering the promised cure. This shift in perspective was not a sign of defeat, but a necessary change in tactics. Rather than battling my body, I needed to listen to it, to work with it.

This is where the power of words became crucial. I no longer saw cancer as an enemy to be eradicated but as a condition to be understood, a part of my body's story. The language I used to describe my illness and my treatment had to evolve. Words like "battle" and "kill" only added stress, fear, and aggression. Instead, I began to use words that aligned with healing, harmony, and balance. I sought to create an environment, both within myself and around me, that supported my entire being—physical, emotional, mental and spiritual.

And as I aligned my words with my intentions, it felt as though the Universe heard me. Slowly, things began to shift. The energy around me changed. What I needed came into my life, as if the very act of choosing different words had set new wheels in motion. My journey wasn't just about surviving cancer anymore; it was about reclaiming my being, not through fighting, but through understanding. Through words that heal, not harm.

CHAPTER 22

"There's a place for traditional medicine, but the true healing begins when we learn to harness the mind's power. Together, the body and mind become allies in the healing process, allowing us to go beyond what medicine alone can achieve."

- Dr. Joe Dispenza

Unbeknownst to me, the disease had been quietly advancing, progressing while I rested in a false sense of security. The side effects of chemotherapy had subsided, and I clung to the belief that my clean-living regimen—nutritious eating, restful sleep, and meditation—would be enough to heal me completely. For a time, I convinced myself that sheer willpower, faith, and a holistic lifestyle could overcome anything. But life, in its wisdom, had other lessons in store for me.

My relentless teacher—the disease—pulled me back into a place of humility, forcing me to confront truths I had overlooked. I had experienced what felt like a miracle just months before, a profound moment I set aside as if it could wait for later reflection. Empowered by that experience, I began to believe that my determination alone could conquer even cancer. I let myself drift into a mindset where I dismissed the very medical system that had once saved my life. I labeled chemotherapy as "poison" and ignored a fundamental truth: while I am indeed a spiritual being, I also inhabit a physical body—a vessel that requires care and attention as much as the spirit within.

I had leaned too heavily into the metaphysical, focusing on the subtle, energetic self while neglecting the pressing physical reality of the disease still within me. It is true that we are spiritual beings having a human experience, but that experience is intricately tied to the health and functionality of our physical bodies. When our vessels falter, they require the tools and expertise of physical medicine to heal—tools that cannot be replaced by spiritual practices alone.

This journey has taught me the importance of balance. True healing lies in honoring both the physical and energetic aspects of our being. One does not replace the other; instead, they work together in harmony. Physical medical care provides the foundation for addressing acute issues, while the subtle energy body holds the key to deeper emotional and spiritual wellness. Together, they form the whole picture of health—one that I could no longer afford to overlook.

Reality came crashing in on the afternoon of August 15, 2023. While preparing for a Zoom call with a friend, a wave of dizziness struck me. I had felt "off" for days but couldn't quite articulate it. It was as though I had vertigo, though not exactly. This time, it was worse. I managed to cut the call short and climb the stairs to my room, where the dizziness intensified. Panic set in as I realized I had no control over my body.

In my fear, I called my friend Rocio, who arrived within minutes. The look on her face said it all—I wasn't well. She called Juliana and Vanja, two other friends, who came as quickly as they could. Juliana reached out to her mother, a naturopathic doctor, who suggested a remedy for vertigo, but the medicine was an hour away by boat in Panajachel. With the lake boats unavailable so late at night, we had to make do with what we had.

My friends worked tirelessly to help me, massaging pressure points, using an "electrical egg" device for inflammation, and giving me Bach flower remedies. They made tea, toast, and—most importantly—stayed by my side. Despite their efforts, the dizziness persisted. That night, we had an impromptu sleepover, their presence a comfort amid my distress.

But as much as I wanted to believe in the power of holistic healing, I couldn't deny the truth: it wasn't enough. My AML was too advanced. No amount of herbs, energy work, or good intentions could undo the physical damage. I needed medical intervention, whether I liked it or not.

When I finally returned to the city and had blood work done, the results were terrifying. My hemoglobin levels were dangerously low, explaining the unrelenting dizziness. My brother, seeing the results, was quick to act. His urgency made one thing clear: my time in Guatemala was over. Its private, expensive healthcare system could no longer meet my needs. Only the best medical care could help me now, and that meant leaving.

Fortunately—or perhaps fatefully—I had already planned a trip to the U.S. for September 6, 2023. The trip, initially meant to join Canche and Ricky on a celebratory European vacation, became my lifeline. My brother arranged for a life-saving blood transfusion that raised my hemoglobin enough to make the journey possible.

Amid all this, my brother's reaction surprised me the most. Always the strong, composed one, he broke down, his vulnerability laid bare. At a farewell dinner he hosted for me, he pulled me aside, teary-eyed, urging me to focus on my bucket list. His words hit hard, but I didn't cry. Not because I lacked emotion but because his perspective, though steeped in love and concern, didn't align with mine.

While he seemed resigned to the realities of my condition, I had learned a deeper lesson: acceptance. True acceptance isn't surrender; it's a deliberate choice, a state of peace that replaces fear with hope and regret with joy. With acceptance came gratitude, the ultimate lesson. Gratitude transformed my perspective, shifting my focus from scarcity to abundance, from fear to trust.

As I prepared to leave, my brother mentioned MD Anderson—a whisper that became a beacon. Known as one of the top cancer centers in the U.S., and located in Houston, Texas, it offered a thread of hope. My focus shifted once again, this time with renewed clarity and purpose.

This was not the end but a turning point, and I was ready to move forward.

PART 4

CHAPTER 23

"Healing isn't linear
It's a journey and a quest
To remember the spiritual
self and awaken to your
best"
"Today I choose to
remember
That within me is pure
love
From January till
December
I welcome in help from up
above"
"Healing isn't linear it
happens in the Now
Today I choose to live in
health
Remembering my
wholeness is the epitome
of wealth."

– Kyle Gray

As I mentioned before, I had already experienced what I believed to be a miracle. While I hold faith in miracles, I've often felt a sense of skepticism about being worthy of receiving one myself. This doubt wasn't solely rooted in feelings of unworthiness; it also stemmed from how the miracle was framed—through Jesus Christ.

I've always wrestled with this depiction, not because I don't believe in Jesus, but because my understanding of Him has evolved into something far more expansive and inclusive than the traditional religious portrayal. My connection with Christ has been deeply personal, beginning with my Catholic upbringing and later growing through my study of the New Testament, the Dead Sea Scrolls, and historical accounts of Jesus. Books like *The Universal Christ* by Fr. Richard Rohr illuminated a vision of Christ as a divine presence encompassing all creation, far beyond the confines of religion.

The idea of "being saved in Jesus' name" has always felt narrow to me. It raised the unsettling question: What about the countless people who aren't Christian? Are they excluded from grace? For years, this exclusivity troubled me, as it seemed at odds with the universal love and boundless compassion I believed Christ embodies.

In late August 2023, as my health deteriorated and fear gripped me, I realized I couldn't face the journey ahead alone. I needed to turn to God—to a Christ who transcends religious boundaries, a presence infinitely divine and deeply personal. In that moment of surrender, I found solace not in the Jesus bound to doctrine but in the Christ who meets each of us wherever we are, without conditions.

Within the comforting walls of my mother's devout Catholic household, surrounded by sacred images and my family's unwavering faith, I sought healing. I reached out to a priest for the sacrament of anointing, leaning into a tradition that had always been part of my life, yet now felt new. My mother had transformed my old bedroom into a small chapel, adorned with statues of Jesus, Mary, angels, and a cherished image of Archangel Michael. Among these was a drawing I've always loved—*Jesus the Healer,* showing Him tenderly caring for a woman holding her child.

This image, which once hung in my father's clinic, speaks to the Christ I hold close to my heart: a presence of healing, love, and inclusion—not confined to suffering on the cross but alive in the fullness of divine compassion. It is this Christ, vast and universal, who has walked with me through my fears and struggles, reminding me that true salvation lies not in exclusivity but in the all-encompassing embrace of love.

The priest came to our home, listened to my story, and offered to hear my confession. I hadn't participated in this sacrament since I was a child, as I had always struggled with the idea of needing a "middleman" to connect with God. But in that moment of illness and fear, I found solace in the ritual. After my confession, the priest asked my family to gather in the chapel for a shortened version of the Sunday gospel reading and to take Communion, the Body of Christ.

As soon as I took the sacrament, an incredible sense of relief washed over me. In that moment, I *knew* I would be okay. I had no doubt that I would make it through, that I would be able to seek out other avenues for healing in a specialized medical setting.

From that point forward, synchronicities began to unfold, one after the other, guiding me toward the path I needed to follow. The presence of a greater power was undeniable, and I understood that I was not walking this journey alone.

CHAPTER 24

"Buddhist teachings explain, 'You can search
the whole universe and not find any being
more worthy of love than yourself.'"

– Jack Kornfield, "The Wise Heart"

Synchronicities began to abound one after another...now I called them miracles

First Miracle:

At the time, my health was so fragile that the thought of traveling—was daunting. Managing airports with a severely compromised immune system seemed like a nearly insurmountable task. I knew I needed help, so I requested wheelchair assistance from the airline, but the prospect of traveling alone still felt precarious.

Then, something remarkable happened. My younger sister's boss, by sheer coincidence, was booked on the exact same flight I was taking from Guatemala to Houston. She offered to keep an eye on me during the flight, which was already a great relief. But when she learned that Houston wasn't my final destination—that I was headed to San Antonio—she went above and beyond. Using her own frequent flier miles, she purchased a ticket for my sister to accompany me all the way to San Antonio, ensuring I arrived safely.

It was no small thing. The synchronicity of having someone connected to my family on the very same flight, the generosity of her gesture, and the fact that it came when I was at my most vulnerable felt like an undeniable sign that I was being guided and protected. This act of kindness made what seemed like an overwhelming journey into something manageable, giving me both the physical support and the emotional reassurance that I wasn't alone.

Second Miracle:

Despite Canche and Ricky spending two years searching for a house in San Antonio, the housing market became so inflated that it slipped beyond their financial reach. So, they decided to rent a house while they figured out where to look for a more reasonable market, not necessarily in San Antonio as my son wasn't too keen on staying here as a permanent resident.

As it turned out, San Antonio is home to a branch of MD Anderson. This discovery was a game changer. The San Antonio facility, though smaller than the one in Houston, actually offers an advantage—its size allows for a more intimate, personalized level of care. The medical team here is able to focus on patients with a level of attention that can sometimes be lost in larger hospitals.

And here was the true stroke of synchronicity: the MD Anderson center in San Antonio is located just a 20-minute drive from my son's home. It felt as though all the obstacles they'd faced in trying to buy a house had led to this moment, aligning perfectly with my need for specialized care. Had they moved elsewhere or even found a home farther from the city, this invaluable proximity to such a top-tier medical facility wouldn't have been possible. There was no longer any need for me to travel all the way to Houston. The care I needed was practically on my doorstep, making my treatment journey smoother and more manageable.

Third Miracle:

The wait for my first appointment at MD Anderson was agonizingly long and fraught with stress. Despite having submitted all the required paperwork, test results, and an exhaustive history of my previous treatments, weeks passed without any progress. Meanwhile, my health took a sharp and alarming turn for the worse, just as my brother had feared. My hemoglobin levels plummeted to a critical 5, forcing an emergency rush to the ER at a nearby hospital.

At the hospital, I was given three units of blood, but even after the transfusions, the attending doctor refused to discharge me. My condition was far too fragile, and he insisted I could only leave if I secured care at another hospital under the supervision of an oncologist. Because the oncologist at this particular hospital left me deeply unsettled. His demeanor lacked the confidence and reassurance I desperately needed in such a precarious moment. I felt uneasy and unheard, as though my condition wasn't being taken with the seriousness it warranted.

The ER itself added to my unease. Overcrowded and chaotic, it didn't even have a private room to shield me from potential infections—a grave risk given my severely compromised immune system. I felt trapped, both physically vulnerable and emotionally adrift, with no clear solution to stabilize my worsening condition.

In this moment of desperation, my son took a bold step. He reached out to a friend who had recently lost her father to the same type of leukemia I was battling. Despite her grief, she spoke with heartfelt praise about her father's oncologist and urged my son to contact her without hesitation. It was a glimmer of hope in an otherwise bleak and terrifying situation.

Sitting at my bedside in the ER, my son composed a lengthy email, explaining the dire situation and pleading for help. It was a shot in the dark, and he feared it might go unanswered. But to our immense relief, the oncologist responded swiftly. She immediately took action, arranging for my transfer to University Hospital, where she was an attending physician and affiliated with MD Anderson!

This response felt like a lifeline. The speed and care with which the oncologist acted not only got me out of a deeply uncomfortable and unsafe situation in the ER but also secured the specialized care I had been waiting for. I finally felt a sense of hope and reassurance, knowing I was in the hands of someone who understood the urgency and complexity of my condition. What had begun as a desperate plea for help turned into another moment of synchronicity, guiding me toward the care I so desperately needed.

Fourth Miracle:

I was admitted to the hospital for 10 days, during which time I underwent a bone marrow biopsy—an excruciatingly painful procedure. The results were devastating: more than 70% of my bone marrow was infiltrated with cancerous cells. The gap in time without chemotherapy had allowed the disease to spread rapidly, which is what makes AML so dangerous— the "A" stands for "Acute," and in my case, the disease had progressed aggressively.

The oncologist, known for her direct communication, didn't mince words. She informed me that without treatment, I was looking at mere months of life, not years. How many months, she couldn't say, but the prognosis was grim. However, she swiftly devised a plan of action, placing me on a treatment protocol of azacitidine combined with venetoclax (Venclexta). This regimen is specifically designed for older AML patients or those who, like me, are unable to endure the intensity of induction chemotherapy—the kind of aggressive treatment I had previously received in Guatemala.

Guatemala, unfortunately, has no access to these newer medications, especially venetoclax, which is cutting-edge in AML treatment. Even if it were available, it would only be accessible to those able to pay exorbitant amounts. To give perspective, a 28-day supply of venetoclax costs around $3,500—a price completely out of reach for most people. This treatment option simply didn't exist for me back home, making my arrival in San Antonio and enrollment in this protocol yet another stroke of fortune.

Despite the severity of my condition, I responded remarkably well to the treatment. The combination of azacitidine and venetoclax began working quickly. The timing of my transfer to this hospital, the access to these advanced treatments, and my body's positive response all lined up in a way that felt nothing short of miraculous. Each step, each new protocol, brought me closer to hope in a situation that had seemed so hopeless.

Fifth Miracle:

In Guatemala, I had no health insurance, and although my doctors generously waived their fees as a professional courtesy to my brother, the costs of my treatments were overwhelming. Hospitalizations, biopsies, lab work, and medications quickly added up to insurmountable sums. Thankfully, the kindness and generosity of Canche, Ricky, and many dear friends, along with a "Go Fund Me" campaign, helped ease the financial burden. I remain profoundly grateful for their support.

In July, while still residing at the Four Pillars in San Pablo la Laguna, I applied for Medicare coverage after turning 65—the qualifying age. The timing couldn't have been more miraculous. Though I don't clearly recall how I connected with "Medicare Joe," his assistance was nothing short of a godsend. He guided me through the complexities of the Medicare process, providing invaluable advice. However, there was one crucial stipulation: I had to reside in the United States to qualify for coverage.

By the time I arrived in San Antonio in early September, frail and in urgent need of intensive, costly medical care, I was fully covered by Medicare—a lifeline that came just in time. But the miracles didn't stop there. The hospital where I received treatment had a charity program, and my oncologist and medical team took the initiative to submit my application. The result was extraordinary: my out-of-pocket costs for the entire hospitalization, including treatments, medications, and the prohibitively expensive venetoclax, amounted to an astounding $0.

It was nothing short of a financial miracle. In Guatemala, I had been drowning under the weight of medical bills I couldn't pay, relying on the goodwill of others. Here, in the United States, I suddenly had access to world-class care without the looming fear of financial devastation. The combination of Medicare and the hospital's charity program lifted an immense burden from my shoulders, allowing me to focus solely on healing. For the first time in a long while, I could breathe deeply, free from the anxiety of debt, and so could my loved ones.

Sixth Miracle:

As I previously mentioned, I responded exceptionally well to the treatment protocol prescribed by my new oncologist. She explained that this regimen of azacitidine and venetoclax could potentially continue indefinitely, managing the leukemia and keeping it in remission. However, she also made it clear that the best path toward a potential "cure," rather than just remission, would be to undergo a bone marrow transplant. A transplant offered the possibility of eradicating the disease entirely, not just keeping it at bay.

With that in mind, my oncologist took swift action and arranged for me to meet with a renowned expert in the field, Dr. Beyhar Zoghi. He came highly recommended and had an impressive reputation. Not only had he been named a Texas Super Doctor from 2019 to 2023, but he also received outstanding reviews from patients who praised his attentiveness, compassion, and dedication. What truly resonated with me, though, was his holistic approach to healing. Dr. Zoghi emphasized the importance of treating both the body and the soul, embodying the Methodist Healthcare philosophy. "If you help the patient by combining the spiritual and the physical—the entire person—it's very rewarding," he explained.

On November 29, 2023, I had my first consultation with Dr. Zoghi. He walked me through the intricacies of the bone marrow transplant process, which, to be honest, could scare the life out of anyone. The procedure is complex, and the risks are real. But Dr. Zoghi's calm and reassuring demeanor made all the difference. He explained that, given my health otherwise, I was an excellent candidate for the transplant. At 65, I was considered "young" and, crucially, I had no other comorbidities that would complicate the procedure. Moreover, he pointed out that my body had already shown a tendency to relapse, making the transplant not just a preferable option but a necessary one.

Dr. Zoghi's words gave me hope. The transplant was the best chance I had at potentially overcoming AML for good. It felt like yet another miracle—an opportunity for a new lease on life. With his expertise, combined with his spiritual approach to care, I felt confident that I was in the right hands to pursue this life-saving option.

"My wonderful doctor Behyar Zoghi, MD, PhD, FACP and me for Halloween 2024"

Seventh Miracle:

As I embarked on a healing journey that involved targeted chemotherapy and the anticipation of a bone marrow transplant, it became clear that I would be staying in San Antonio for quite some time. Initially, I was living with Canche and Ricky, but space quickly became an issue. With only one bathroom to share and me sleeping in my son's office/studio, things began to feel crowded and less comfortable for everyone. Though we share a deep love for one another, we were all aware of the need for personal space, especially with the stressful situation we were in.

When I left Guatemala, I was so ill that I didn't even pack my own luggage. Everything I owned was left behind, and I arrived in the U.S. with just a small suitcase of clothes. It was another lesson in non-attachment, learning to let go of material things and focus on what truly mattered—my health. However, this meant I had very little to start with in terms of personal belongings or setting up a new space.

Just as I was deciding to move forward with Dr. Zoghi and his transplant team, another stroke of luck presented itself. The little house, or "casita," that sits on the same property as my son's home suddenly became available for rent. The casita was normally rented out as an Airbnb, so it was fully furnished and equipped with everything I would need, down to the kitchen utensils. The property owner had always appreciated how well Canche and Ricky took care of their place, and when we expressed interest in renting the casita, she was thrilled to have me as a new tenant.

Of course, there was no way I could afford the rent on my own. But here's where the timing of everything felt like another miracle. Canche and Ricky, who have been supporting me financially since my time in Guatemala, had just finished paying off their car in November—right when the casita became available. This freed up their finances, and they generously offered to help cover my rent partially. Between the three of us, we split the rent equally, making it possible for me to live independently and comfortably, without the need to buy a single item to furnish the space.

The availability of the casita, fully equipped and ready for me, felt like the universe aligning once again to provide exactly what was needed at just the right moment. It gave me the peace and privacy I needed during such a critical time in my treatment, and it allowed Canche and Ricky to have their space as well. More than just a physical place, the casita became a sanctuary, a reminder that even in the midst of uncertainty, there are moments of grace and provision that make the path forward a little smoother.

CHAPTER 25

"In the practical order of life, if we have never loved deeply or suffered deeply, we are unable to understand spiritual things at any depth. Any healthy and "true" religion is teaching you how to deal with the suffering and how to deal with love. And if you allow this process with sincerity, you will soon recognize that it is actually love and suffering that are dealing with you, like nothing else can! Even God has to use love and suffering to teach you all the lessons that really matter. They are His primary tools for human transformation."

- Fr. Richard Rohr, "The Universal Christ"

The Greatest Miracle

At precisely 12:52 p.m. on January 31, 2024, I received an email from the transplant coordinator delivering the most incredible news: Canche, my beloved son, had qualified to be my primary bone marrow donor.

For as long as I can remember, I've always said that Canche and I share a symbiotic relationship. We've spent a lifetime lifting each other up in moments of despair, offering strength and courage when one of us was lacking. In recent years, I've found myself leaning on him more and more. But the beauty of our connection is that it has always been a two-way street—a dance of mutual support and unwavering love.

When I was just 17, I felt a deep, divine calling to bring this precious life into the world, against all odds. I faced social rejection, humiliation, and the heavy burden of being ostracized. My decision came at a great personal cost. I was denied a higher education, married under difficult circumstances, and endured many years of hardship, including the painful loss of myself in the process. Yet, here we are now, decades later, standing together in an unbreakable bond.

The child I brought into the world at such a tender age is now a healthy, strong 47-year-old man, and he is about to give me the most sacred gift—the gift of life. He is giving me his stem cells to restore my failing bone marrow. How poetic and beautiful is that? The very being I gave life to is now, in turn, giving life back to me.

It doesn't escape me that he too is facing his own struggles, particularly in feeling "trapped" in a place where he doesn't quite feel like he belongs, unable to fully conform. He is sacrificing a part of himself for me, just as I once did for him. I've often called Canche my "angel" because of his pure, angelic presence, and now more than ever, I see how divinely orchestrated his role in my life has been. For this, I thank God with all my heart for sending me this beautiful angel.

On March 27, 2024, I received the ultimate gift—fresh, healthy stem cells to bring me back to life. This miraculous transplant, made possible by the love and sacrifice of my son, has given me a second chance at life, a chance to be whole again. The journey has come full circle.

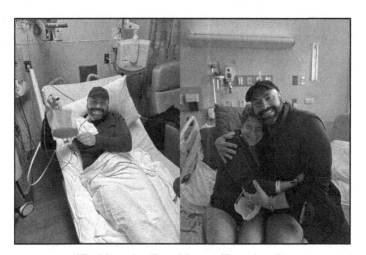

*"The Miraculous Bone Marrow Transplant Day
at Methodist Hospital on March 27, 2024"*

This is where my story reaches its conclusion, it's not a self-help guide on facing a life-threatening diagnosis, nor is it a how-to manual on surviving a bone marrow transplant. For me, the process has already been a success, a miracle. This is a testimony to the power of faith, the reward of acceptance, the strength of free will, and the courage that comes from deep self-discovery. Above all, it is a testament to the highest and most powerful force in the universe—love.

Throughout my journey with AML, faith and prayer have been my constant companions. Prayer groups formed around me, filled with people offering their purest intentions, best wishes, and an overwhelming outpouring of love for my healing. The support I have received from these individuals has been nothing short of awe-inspiring. Their love and positive energy has been a tangible force, a collective connection that has uplifted me during my darkest moments.

At the beginning of this journey, I embraced the belief that I chose this life—the time and place of my birth, my gender, my socio-economic status, and even the people who would become my family. I believe I consciously selected these circumstances for a profound reason, even if that purpose was initially unclear.

As I walked this path, the veils of illusion began to lift, revealing truths I had long overlooked. I realized that I had not been truly living; I had merely been surviving. And there is a vast difference between the two. I began to understand that the true journey of healing was an ongoing process, a movement toward deeper truths and self-awareness.

It is through suffering that I found the truth, though my beloved books and wise teachers have been an invaluable source and have played their part. The real Truth, with a capital T, emerged not from facts or intellectual inquiry but from the felt sense that has been with me since childhood—a knowing that resides in the heart, not in the mind. The Ultimate Teacher, life itself, led me to acceptance and gratitude. It awakened me to the abundant generosity and love that poured into my life, revealing the undeniable presence of a Higher Power working through me.

Gratitude, generosity, forgiveness, compassion—these are the lessons I have gained since my diagnosis, and they are all qualities of the heart, not the mind. My heart, which knew these truths from an early age, has expanded through life's trials, experiences, and acquired wisdom. The Ultimate Teacher allowed me to grasp this knowledge in a profound and deeply felt way, and for that, I am immensely grateful.

In my quest to know myself, I've come to reflect on the profound gift of life that has been extended to me through the bone marrow transplant. Beyond gratitude, I feel a stirring within, a call to be of service to humanity. However, I now understand that this service is not about doing, but about being. It is about embodying the light, the spark of life that I received in the form of my son's cells.

That spark, born from complete love and surrender, is the essence of the life I have been given. It is now my duty to carry that light forward, to shine it brightly into the world.

And so, the greatest miracle is not just the healing of my body, but the profound awakening of my soul—the realization that I have been, and always will be, a vessel of love and light. Now, it's time to let that light shine forward, illuminating the path for others as I continue to walk my own.

Today, I find myself sitting at my beautiful desk, writing—my favorite activity—on a brand-new computer gifted by my loving son last Christmas, a holiday we once feared might be my last. And yet, here I am, against all odds. Despite the challenges my body, mind, and soul have endured, I'm here. The truth is, I don't quite understand how it all came together.

I don't fully grasp the science behind the intricate process of a bone marrow transplant or the complex workings within this miraculous vessel we call the body. But somehow, every medication, every procedure, worked—and here I am, writing my much anticipated memoir.

Maybe it's the mystery of not knowing that makes life so extraordinary. For years, I felt the need to know everything—an expectation I held as a teacher. Admitting I didn't have all the answers felt almost unacceptable. But over time, I realized that not knowing allowed me to keep an open, curious mind, one eager to embrace new ideas and absorb the endless things there are to learn.

Gradually, saying "I don't know" became not only acceptable but liberating. It allowed me to see the world through a child's eyes—wide open and in awe.

Dacher Keltner, a scientist and author, describes awe as an experience of embracing mystery, connecting us deeply to the unknown and helping us "appreciate what is most humane in our human nature." This openness to life's mysteries brought a sense of humility and trust. Perhaps these qualities became vital ingredients in the complex equation that has kept me alive a little longer. For how long?

I don't know!

Acknowledgements

None of this book would have been possible without the celestial intervention and divine timing of the people, places and events that aided me along my path. It gives me immense pleasure to at least give a nod of acknowledgment here.

Starting with my ancestors. I want to say thank you and I see you, even those whom I did not have the opportunity to make their acquaintance with. However, it is because of ALL of you saying 'yes' to life all the way down to my parents, that I eventually sprouted along this same bloodline. Thank you to my paternal grandparents Olga and Miguel Angel, who loved me unconditionally and swooped in to take care of me whenever I was in need. Thank you to my maternal grandparents, Zoila and Victor, whom I didn't have the opportunity to get to know well but I thank you for allowing your love to give rise to my beautiful mother. Thank you to my parents who did their best to provide me with so much love. Thank you dad for instilling in me that thirst for knowledge that is never truly quenched in me. And a very special thank you to you mom - whom at age 85 - your light still shines bright! I am so grateful to have you on this earthly plane. Not just full of life but full of the Joy of life. Your eternal positivity, generosity and unbending faith is surely one of the main reasons I am still around. Thank you for being the sacred portal from which I came into this world. I love you beyond measure!

An eternal and soulful "thank you" to my beloved son Canche not just for those life saving stem cells you generously and so lovingly offered to me but also for the million and one thing and a half that you do for me each and everyday! I truly don't know what I would do without you. You are my rock where I stand firmly on, my shoulder where I can rest my head upon and my loving confidant. You truly are a Godsend. And, the same sentiment goes to Ricky, your beloved life partner who has been a true and close friend to me always and in these precarious times even more so. Thank you for everything, for those delicious meals, for the laughter, for your understanding, your genuine care and affection towards me and for the beautiful book cover you designed! I owe so much to the both of you that "thank you" doesn't seem to cover the entire sentiment.

Thank you to my daughter Beba who took care of me and documented those first days of treatment so well and so beautifully. Your amazing talent in storytelling through photography was the basis for a much needed GoFundMe movement that assisted me so much. And especially thank you for that loving embrace in the shower when I lost all my hair and for holding my hand in the hospital when the pain of the needles was too much to bear. You were there for me when I needed you most and I will always treasure that. I love you for eternity.

Thank you to my beautiful son Danny for dropping everything and coming to Guatemala to keep me company during those long days after chemo in isolation in my apartment in Los Rincones. You also took on the task of administering the dreaded Filgrastim injections and taking care of my eye with so much tenderness when I developed that infection. And specially thank you for the delicious brownies you baked for me on a weekly basis. I will always treasure our deep conversations and our shared humor. I love you to infinity and beyond!

Thank you to the medical establishment both in Guatemala City at Hospital Centro Medico as well as in San Antonio, Texas. Starting with my brother, Miguel, who from the very beginning took on the reins of arranging a medical team of specialists to confront this disease in the best way possible. Thank you Lito, my dear brother, for it was in deference to you that I was cared for so generously. And by extension, thank you to your loving wife Ani, for opening her house and her heart to take care of me when I needed it so much. And a HUGE thank you to Dr. Elizabeth Bowhay-Carnes, the oncologist who saved me when I arrived in Texas and who then referred me to the astounding and most graceful Dr. Beyhar Zoghi who poured in all his knowledge and genuine care to assist in giving me my life back. And of course, to all the nursing staff, lab technicians, and dutiful administrators of the Texas Transplant Physicians Group Blood and Marrow Transplant Program at Methodist Hospital in San Antonio, Texas. You ALL have been very special to me and I forever will be grateful for all your tender love and care.

Thank you to my sisters, Ginna and Myriam, who both stepped in immediately to offer me anything and everything you could do to alleviate me. Thank you Ginna, my unconditional supporter, for all those trips back and forth to the hospital and to the doctor's clinic and especially thank you for taking up the task in administering those Filgrastim injections, you made the pain go away with your warmth and laughter. And, thank you Myriam for being my much needed travel companion when I was too weak and scared. Your lightness of heart and your beautiful disposition made me always feel safe and loved. I love the both of you SO much!

To all the friends that replied to the call of distress and who were by my side, perhaps not always physically, but soulfully which is even more special. To my childhood friends, thank you for coming back into my life after so many years of not seeing each other, yet ready and attentive to come to my aid when I needed it. To Brande and Josh who assisted with the creation of the GoFundMe page and for all your love and visits in Guatemala City, at Lake Atitlan and for that special birthday/100 day post transplant celebration in San Antonio. Your company is always a fun treasure. To my dearest friend Nancy who also came to visit me prior to the transplant and gave me so much strength and grace to go through with it in a positive light. I love our daily communications and our growing friendship. To my sweet and beautiful friend Diann who is always an attentive ear and a wise companion in sharing our interest in all things esoteric, especially the teachings of William Meader, our conversations after each webinar are so uplifting. To Liz and Brian for their much needed and much appreciated support in Chicago and beyond. I love you all.

Thank you to the beautiful people of San Pablo la Laguna, Atitlan. Especially to Mark Elmy for entrusting me with your beautiful property "The Four Pillars" - that enchanted house was central to my path on this journey. You made my dream of living at Lake Atitlan come true. And especially thank you for that heartfelt Mayan ceremony you held for my special day - 1 Kej - I believe it gave me the strength needed to take on all the challenges that were about to come my way. Thank you to Rocio and her beautiful children Pau and Ceiba who I love dearly. Especially thank you for entrusting me with their education and for coming to my aid when I desperately needed it and on more than one occasion. Thank you to Juliana and Vanja, my adored friends who gave me the best therapy sessions and who became my most trusted companions. Thank you for all the laughter, the joy and those special dinners we shared and for staying connected even with all the miles between us. Thank you to Pedro, Rosario, Loida, Javier and the many other beautiful people of San Pablo who took care of me in many different and loving ways. I love you all so very, very much!

Thank you to Vivian Solis, my warm and wise therapist who combines science and spirituality with such grace. I have learned so much from you! And to the Vivi Moradas Group, your wise counsel and loving attention to what was happening brought me to accept the miracles that were coming my way. Thank you for introducing me to A Course in Miracles. I'm always in a state of gratitude for our connection that was aided so lovingly by the mystery of the Universe which is always timely and always true. Thank you!

And last but never ever least, thank you to my constant and loving companion Archangel Michael, your palpable and powerful presence has been felt by my soul since my childhood and without you I would be lost. THANK YOU - THANK YOU - THANK YOU for always being by my side protecting me when I need it, guiding me along the path of life, but mostly just loving me unconditionally and showing me that I AM never alone.